A Reformer's Art

Fanny and Little Dorrit Call on Mrs. Merdle

Hablot Browne, Frontispiece to *Little Dorrit*

A Reformer's Art

Dickens' Picturesque and Grotesque Imagery

NANCY K. HILL

Ohio University Press
ATHENS · LONDON

Library of Congress Cataloging in Publication Data

Hill, Nancy K 1936–
A reformer's art.

Bibliography: p.
Includes index.
1. Dickens, Charles, 1812–1870–Criticism and interpretation.
2. Dickens, Charles, 1812–1870–Political and social views. 3. Grotesque in literature. I. Title. II. Title: Picturesque and grotesque imagery.
PR4581.H54 823'.8 80-23256
ISBN 0-8214-0586-1
ISBN 0-8214-0613-2 pbk.

Printed in the United States of America.

To my mother
Helen Crooker Klenk
and my mother-in-law
Ruth Davis Hill

Acknowledgements

WHEN A working mother sets out to write a book on Dickens, she can scarcely avoid the fear that her household may degenerate to the condition of Mrs. Jellyby's, and her project amount to little more than Borrioboola-Gha. The patterns I had witnessed were not encouraging.

My mother, who first read Dickens to me when I was a small child, had been among the first exchange students to France, and one of the very few to win a degree from a French university. She gave up teaching to marry my father during the depression, and hid her Phi Beta Kappa key in a drawer. In a pattern consonant with the nineteenth century she abandoned her own aspirations in order to devote full time to her house and children, but I often sensed she had paid dearly for her choice.

My mother-in-law, on the other hand, worked full time in the family business, served for 18 years on the school board, and maintained a tasteful, orderly home—with the assistance of both full and part-time help.

When, under the kindly direction of Jean H. Hagstrum at Northwestern, I began the dissertation that led to this book, I had two small children in a Chicago apartment. I had no full-time help, nor the prospect of any, but I had Roscoe Hill. My remarkable husband has over the years not only managed an increasingly demanding professional career, but has encouraged and enabled me to develop one as well.

That our home does not resemble Mrs. Jellyby's owes much to the unstinting efforts of my husband and the helpfulness of our children, Stephen and Jenny. If this book belongs to Borrioboola-Gha, it is no fault of my precious family's.

Nor is it the fault of my friends and colleagues who have read my work in various stages: James Kincaid, Robert Richardson, Richard Schoeck, Hazel Barnes, and James Palmer.

I am grateful to the Beinecke Library for allowing me to use the Holbein print from "The Alphabet of Death" and to *Hartford Studies in Literature* for allowing me to use material on the picturesque which first appeared in an article there.

Illustrations from Dickens' novels are taken from the Oxford Illustrated Dickens. Holbein illustrations from *The Dance of Death* are taken from the Dover edition (New York, 1971). Hogarth illustrations are from Ronald Paulson, *Hogarth's Graphic Works,* 2 vols. (New Haven: Yale University Press, 1965) and from Paulson, *Hogarth: His Life, Art and Times* (New Haven: Yale University Press, 1971).

Contents

List of Illustrations

Introduction: Visual Imagery and Moral Reform

THE VICTORIAN Age, perhaps more than any other period, valued the visual image, a fact we have only recently begun to acknowledge. As we brush the cobwebs off our recollected portraits of great granny in her stern posture and fussy frame, we begin to perceive that our earlier impressions of the Victorian aesthetic did not enable us to understand the period very well. Now a wealth of material on Victorian art and architecture is pouring forth, and the process of re-evaluation is well under way.

Departmentalized as our universities have become, students of English have been unapprised that Victorians considered the visual arts to be literature's sister.[1] A remarkable unanimity of purpose characterized the sister arts as poets and painters recognized the power of the visual image to instruct the burgeoning number of people admitted to the world of culture. In this age of didactic purpose and cooperative endeavor in the arts, Charles Dickens emerged as a central figure, one who combined moral purpose and visual imagery in highly persuasive fashion.

Dickens took seeing seriously, even when the visual image elicited laughter, for he knew that our moral responses to the world are determined by our visual perception of it, that we see what we have been taught (by school or custom) to see, and that, if at all possible, we ignore what falls outside our image of the world. The phenomenon he recognized is that which enables residents of Calcutta to walk its foetid streets oblivious to horror, and that which allows Americans to assume their cities are flourishing in spite of mounting statistical evidence to the contrary.

Once an image of a burning building illuminates the TV screen, Americans admit the truth of urban statistics. But it seems to require visual evidence of the world's difference from our illusions to force a change in perception.

This book concerns Dickens' shaping, out of the materials of his time, a visual aesthetic that would alter his readers' perceptions of the world around them. Expressing his ideas through powerfully evocative visual images, Dickens sought not just to entertain, but to instruct, to reform. Dickens wanted his readers to recognize that the world was not just what their limited experience and curtailed perception suggested it was. He wanted them to realize that problems that demanded reform existed in education, in the prisons, in housing, in working conditions. And he wanted to affect their hearts and minds in such a way that they would insist upon change.

To bring about reform, Dickens knew he had to alter his readers' perception, and such alteration required visual imagery of considerable power. In the 1841 preface to his second novel, *Oliver Twist,* Dickens articulates his plan of action:

> It appeared to me that to draw a knot of such associates in crime as really do exist; to paint them in all their deformity, in all their wretchedness, in all the squalid poverty of their lives; to show them as they really are...would be to attempt a something which was greatly needed and which would be a service to society.

Dickens would, as the visual artist does, "draw" and "paint" in order to put before his readers what he later in the preface calls "the miserable reality." Throughout his career he developed a double-edged visual rhetoric intended, on the one hand, to persuade his readers to accept the existence of "the miserable reality," and, on the other hand, to dissuade them from giving much credence to the smugly complacent view of the world perpetrated by the Fine Arts. This book examines that double-edged visual rhetoric: the grotesque imagery intended to widen his readers' awareness of lives outside their own, and the picturesque satire designed to cast doubts on art that did little more than reflect an attitude of ease and comfort.

According to Dickens, the Fine Arts (which he usually capitalized as a mark of contempt) were too genteel, too precious, too removed from the reality of most people's lives. He was disturbed by "the contrast between the polite bearing of the Fine Arts, and the rudeness of real life." Dickens continued in the essay, "An Idea of Mine,"

> I understood now, what I had never understood before, why there were two sentries at the exhibition-door. These are not to be regarded as mere privates in the Foot Guards, but as allegorical personages, stationed there with gun and bayonet to keep out Purpose, and to mount guard over the lassitude of the Fine Arts, laid up in the lavender of other ages.[2]

Dickens perceived a certain narrowness, a certain rigidity, a certain affected prettiness in much contemporary art that interfered with the perception of reality.[3] He believed that contemporary art reflected certain tendencies within the society, and his reading of these visual signs filled him with foreboding.

When he visited the 1855 Paris Exposition, he complained to John Forster that most of the English pictures were painfully methodical:

> There is a horrid respectability about most of the best of them—a little finite, systematic routine in them, strangely expressive to me of the state of England itself.... Don't think it a part of my despondency about public affairs, and my fear that our national glory is on the decline, when I say that mere form and conventionalities usurp, in English art, as in English government and social relations, the place of living force and truth.[4]

In his own work Dickens wanted to create "living force and truth," and he did so by intertwining powerful visual images with an overwhelming sense of commitment to the truth as he understood it. If we try to analyze the resulting moral force, we come very close to Gombrich's "suspicion" that "the feeling of 'truth' or 'sincerity' in art is due to the synesthesia of values."[5]

Dickens' art is a composite, perhaps even a synesthetic, art, which is to say that he conveys ideas through visual images. Those readers who still insist on maiming a novel by "skipping the descriptive" parts miss essential elements of Dickens' created world. His visual imagery carries cognitive meaning, in the sense Rudolph Arnheim has analyzed in *Visual Thinking:*

> My contention is that the cognitive operations called thinking are not the privilege of mental processes above and beyond perception but the essential ingredients of perception itself. I am referring to such operations as active exploration, selection, grasping of essentials, simplification, abstraction, analysis and synthesis, completion, correction, comparison, problem solving, as well as combining, separating, putting in context.[6]

Arnheim argues that visual art is as significant as verbal, that the two are interdependent:

> What we need to acknowledge is that perceptual and pictorial shapes are not only translations of thought products but the very flesh and blood of thinking itself and that an unbroken range of visual interpretation leads from the humble gestures of daily communication to the statements of great art.[7]

Dickens' art exemplifies Arnheim's ideas in many ways. Keenly aware of "the humble gesture," Dickens translates that into great art—and the visual imagery by which he does so is often connected to the visual arts. Not one to present his ideas in the form of a philosophical argument, as George Eliot often does, he clothes his ideas in images, and indeed makes "perceptual and pictorial shapes...the very flesh and blood of thinking itself."

In using verbal pictures to convey meaning, Dickens is not only on solid ground aesthetically, he is also very much a part of his time. The Victorian Age witnessed one of the great recurrences of the sister arts; it was a time when the visual and the verbal arts shared certain common purpose. That purpose was now primarily narrative and realistic, the first criterion giving literature the edge, the second better conveyed through painting.

On varying social levels the special relationship of the arts was expressed. The popular *Illustrated London News* declared at its inception in 1840, "Art...has become the bride of literature," while John Ruskin wrote in *Modern Painters,* 1856, "Painting seems to me only just to be beginning to take its proper place beside literature."[8] Whether visual art is seen as the shy bride standing behind literature, or as a younger sister sitting beside her, requiring intensive guidance, art and literature did enjoy a close relationship in the Victorian period. Indeed, Mario Praz has claimed that "*ut pictura poesis* had become the golden rule—more than it ever had been, more than it ever was to be again—of nineteenth-century narrative literature."[9] The relationship worked both ways, painting taking on a narrative function, and prose fiction describing scenes in pictorial detail.

During his lifetime when painter and novelist shared narrative inclinations, the highest praise Dickens could bestow on his artist friends was to say they would have made equally good writers. When Daniel Maclise died, Dickens eulogized his friend before the Royal Academy of Art: "Of his genius in his chosen art I will venture to say nothing here, but of his prodigious fertility of mind and wonderful wealth of intellect, I may confidently assert that they would have made him, if he had been so minded, at least as great a writer as he was a painter."[10] Dickens held Edwin Landseer in equally high esteem, as is evident from his manner of praising him. "Whenever I speak of men born by nature to be writers if they had not highly distinguished themselves in some other art (they are mighty few) I always instance you with your remarkable powers of observation and perception."[11] And, again, to W.P. Frith, who had evidently written him about his work-in-progress, *The Mystery of Edwin Drood:* "What you write of the murder gives me very high gratification, because *I* know that *you* know what passion and expression *are,* and I esteem your praise accordingly."[12] Dickens assumed that these praiseworthy talents were as applicable to visual as to literary art.

Literature enjoyed the greater prestige, but the desire to express oneself in more than one medium was often heard. Robert Browning concludes his volume *Men and Women* with the wish that he were painter as well as poet—a wish understandable in one who so often described painters and art works in his poetry. Tennyson's poetry contains extensive word-painting (see, especially, "The Palace of Art" and "The Lady of Shalott" that attracted the attention of the Pre-Raphaelites), and Hallam, his most sensitive critic, felt he could best describe the work through analogy to painting. L.M. Findlay, in a wide-ranging article on the sister arts in Victorian criticism, says Hallam "uses the Sister Arts tradition to anchor semiological abstraction in the evocative particulars of art."[13]

In mid-century the Pre-Raphaelites founded *The Germ* which carried the subtitle, "Thoughts toward Nature in Poetry, Literature and Art." It urged potential contributors to express themselves "in another language besides their *own proper* one." Working in this group dedicated to greater unity between the arts, Dante Gabriel Rossetti created works which truly conjoined painting and poetry.

Poets actively concerned with the sister arts could look back at least as far as Horace to a long tradition of *ut pictura poesis.*[14] During the previous century this tradition of seeing a poem as a picture had flowered again, but in the Victorian era prose fiction was the great carrier of the tradition. Thackeray illustrated his own works, sometimes slyly allowing the picture to convey additional meaning not in the text.[15] George Eliot self-consciously adopted an analogy to Dutch genre painting in *Adam Bede,* and Thomas Hardy subtitled *Under the Greenwood Tree* "A Rural Painting of the Dutch School." Reading Victorian fiction, Mario Praz was so struck by the use of genre painting that he took this single element as the key to the period style.

But Dickens is not, as Praz misreads him, primarily a genre painter. His visual rhetoric operates differently from that in *Adam Bede* and *Under the Greenwood Tree* where Dutch genre painting gives a sense of locational sympathy with rural characters. Dickens admired such art, and he particularly admired the nineteenth-century genre painter David Wilkie, but his remarks on the painter indicate a strong rhetorical interest in the effects on the audience created by these works of art.

In an 1841 speech he applauded Wilkie "who made the cottage hearth his grave theme, and who surrounded the lives, and cares, and daily toils and occupations of the poor, with dignity and beauty."[16] His description of his own subject matter in 1842 coincided very nearly with the observations on Wilkie he had made the previous year:

> I believe that Virtue shows quite as well in rags and patches as she does in purple and fine linen. I believe that she and every beautiful object in external nature, claim some sympathy in the breast of the poorest man...I believe...that it is good, and pleasant, and profitable to track her out, and follow her.[17]

In describing the virtue of the poor, Dickens on one occasion drew a picture based on one of Wilkie's models. The scene is in *David Copperfield* where David, visiting the emigrant ship on which Little Em'ly and Mr. Peggotty will sail, "seemed to stand in a picture by OSTADE" (Ch. LVII). The scene develops other correspondences with the Dutch genre painter: the gloom, the "crowded groups of people," the description of small households with few worldly goods. This is traditional literary pictorialism, but rare in Dickens, who generally adapts freely from artistic models without naming or following them closely in detail.

Not only did Dickens make the cottage hearth his theme, but he urged others to do so. He recognized quickly that the new class of art enthusiasts needed instruction, and he pleaded with his fellow artists repeatedly to take upon themselves this task. Speaking at a Literature and Art banquet, Dickens told the assembled artists, "However small the audience, however contracted the circle in the water in the first instance, the people are now the wider range outside; and the Sister Arts, while they instruct them, derive a wholesome advantage and improvement from their ready sympathy and cordial response."[18]

"The wider range" refers to the expanded art audience which developed in the nineteenth century with the opening of the National Gallery and the public's access to works of art previously available to only the wealthy.[19] T.S.R. Boase has remarked on the new public's shift in tastes, and the consequent need for artistic accommodation:

> Painting had long depended on recognizable symbols and the associations of traditional poses for much of its communicative power. For religious and classical themes, or even for portraiture, there was a wealth of allusion, familiar and therefore sufficiently unobtrusive not to diminish the primary impact of the design. The stories told by English painters in the 1830's had no such accepted and enriching iconography. Their points had to be made explicit; it was narration rather than the use of a known convention to crystallize a visual experience.[20]

Dickens' writing career coincides with this expanding public, and he was quickly aware of the new opportunities they provided. He saw his role as one of instructing the public in how to see in order that they should understand. In this he is not merely responding to the currents in his time, but acting in accordance with English tradition. In *The Englishness of English Art,* Pevsner points out that

> to Hogarth art is a medium for preaching and that the most effective sermon is the recounting of what the observant eye sees around. Both are English attitudes. The first is naturally entirely post-medieval; for in the Middle Ages most art was there to preach anyway; the second is eternally English.[21]

Pevsner goes on to suggest that a "preference for observed fact and the personal experience is indeed, as is universally known, the hallmark of English philosophy through the ages."[22]

Dickens, as all are now well aware, had a penchant for direct observation, and he drew repeatedly on his own personal experience—particularly the searing trials of his childhood. He is not idiosyncratic in this, but, as Pevsner shows, in the mainstream of English art, and linked to its best-known artists. "Like Hogarth he was a preacher as well as a painter."[23]

Sometimes he had an actual rostrum from which to address the public. He was often asked by the Royal Academy of Art to deliver the speech at the annual banquet, and he took considerable care to express the high moral purpose shared by the sister arts. Dickens' was one of the strongest voices raised in advocacy of such purpose, and, ironically, but fittingly, his death marked the end of this era of shared purpose.[24]

In his fiction he repeatedly attacks art that fails to meet the standard of moral enlightenment. Such is the art collected by the Dedlocks,

> who have agreed to put a smooth glaze on the world, and to keep down all its realities. For whom everything must be languid and pretty. Who have found out the perpetual stoppage. Who are to rejoice at nothing, and be sorry for nothing. Who are not to be disturbed by ideas. On whom even the Fine Arts, attending in powder and walking backward like the Lord Chamberlain, must array themselves in the milliners' and tailors' patterns of past generations, and be particularly careful not to be in earnest, or to receive any impress from the moving age.[25]

"Fancy-dress portraiture" was a genre in which the rich could indulge, lining their galleries with images of themselves and their ancestors in poses which emphasized costume more than character. If Dickens was caustic concerning the spiritless art surrounding the rich, he was even more satirical regarding the art of the nouveau-riche. In *Our Mutual Friend* he showed that the reduction of art to ever narrower boundaries would ultimately reach the stage he called Podsnappery:

> Mr. Podsnap's notions of the Arts in their integrity might have been stated thus. Literature; large print, respectively descriptive of getting up at eight, shaving close at a quarter-past, breakfasting at nine, going to the City at ten, coming home at half-past five, and dining at seven. Painting and Sculpture; models and portraits representing Professors of getting up at eight, shaving close at a quarter-past, breakfasting at nine, going to the City at ten, coming home at half-past five, and dining at seven.
>
> Ch. XI

Sporadic attacks of this nature are scattered through the fiction and would make an interesting study on their own. The concern of this book, however, is not with the occasional art work in Dickens, but with a shaping aesthetic that determines what art—or reality—one notices at all. During the Victorian era the predominant aesthetic was probably still the picturesque, defined most simply as seeing the world as a picture. In the eighteenth-century heyday of the mode a considerable portion of the English landscape was transformed according to picturesque principles, and in the nineteenth century, town planning developed along the gently curved lines of the picturesque. The eclecticism of the Victorian era flourished under the aegis of the picturesque, but by this time ominous side-effects of this rampant aesthetic were clearly visible to the keen observer—to John Ruskin[26] as well as to Charles Dickens.

Seeing the world in terms of preconceived pictures led to a kind of obtuseness readily ridiculed. And Dickens belittled it in his early fiction. But the phenomenon was more than ridiculous; it was, as Dickens recognized, dangerous for a people to adhere to such a limited set of images. In *Little Dorrit* Dickens mounts a full-scale attack on the picturesque, ground work for this battle having been laid in earlier works. His sustained assault on the picturesque is designed, as his scattered satire on the Fine Arts, to dissuade his readers from retaining a false, complacent way of viewing the world.

To open his readership to realities they had rejected, Dickens employs the grotesque. An extremely complex aesthetic mode, the grotesque combines natural forms in ways not found in nature; it animates the inanimate; it cavorts with the unexpected, the startling, the extraordinary.

Because it establishes a mood of tension and imbalance, grotesque art can be profoundly disquieting and can be used by the serious artist as a means of awakening his readers to social concerns. Angus Fletcher has observed that "when a people is being lulled into inaction by the routine of daily life, so as to forget all higher aspirations, an author perhaps does well to present behavior in a grotesque, abstract caricature. In such a way he may arouse a general self-criticism and the method will be justified."[27]

Dickens' penchant for the grotesque has long been noted, but not as a form of perception necessary to effect reform. Although he suggests this connection, Arthur Clayborough does not go on to develop it:

> The attitude of mind which led Dickens to attack these things [those soulless institutions and theories, the workhouse, the law, the factory, commercialism, Benthamism, and so on] is in large measure related to his intense awareness and appreciation of the *peculiarities* of human nature as they manifest themselves in appearance, behaviour, and speech.[28]

Dickens' "attack" and his awareness are often expressed through grotesque imagery.

It is my contention that Dickens developed a visual rhetoric around these two aesthetic modes, the grotesque and the picturesque, so important in his time. He taught his readers to distrust the surface prettiness that had been presented to them through the picturesque. And, conversely, he taught his readers, by means of the grotesque, to probe for meaning below, or between, the surfaces. While the picturesque, by its pleasing array of elements calls forth a disengaged appreciation of vistas, the grotesque, by its incongruous combination of elements, elicits a disquieting sense of apprehension. The moral sense has little contact with the disengaged, but it can operate within the disquieted. Dickens as moralist is more preoccupied with the grotesque, and the greater part of this book is given over to the various forms assumed by those conjoined interests. We begin, however, with the opposite pole, with the picturesque that could promise such delight, yet could also convey such deception.

Chapter One
The Picturesque: Delight and Deception

IN *THE Marble Faun* Hawthorne describes with keen appreciation a scene of picturesque beauty:

> They were picturesque in that sweetly impressive way where wildness, in a long lapse of years, has crept over scenes that have been once adorned with the careful art and toil of man; and when man could do no more for them, time and nature came, and wrought hand in hand to bring them to a soft and venerable perfection.
>
> Ch.XXVII

This gentle combination of the cultivated and the wild in mellowing time is the essence of the picturesque, that elusive aesthetic category hovering somewhat uncertainly between the sublime and the beautiful. Perhaps because the wilderness was so proximate to civilization in the new world, the picturesque lingered as a positive aesthetic longer than in England. Thoreau was enchanted by it,[1] and Frederick Law Olmsted planned Central Park according to its principles.[2]

In England the strongest effect of the picturesque was felt in the 18th and early 19th centuries.[3] Landscape values associated with the picturesque occur in the fiction of Mrs. Radcliffe[4] and that of Jane Austen, in the poetry of William Wordsworth, the journals of Dorothy Wordsworth, and the essays of John Ruskin, to cite but a divers few. But there also appeared English satire directed toward the picturesque, satire which intensified during the nineteenth century.

The phenomenon known as the picturesque was recognized rather soon after Burke analyzed the sublime and the beautiful (1757), and it turns up as a descriptive category in the multi-volume Observations of William Gilpin (1724–1804), works which Thoreau read avidly.[5] In "An Essay Upon Prints; containing remarks upon principles of picturesque beauty" (1768), Gilpin defines picturesque as "a term expressive of that peculiar kind of beauty which is agreeable in a picture."[6] In the "Three Essays" he continues to define the picturesque in terms of picture. Early in the essay he distinguishes between the beautiful and the picturesque, "between those, which please the eye in their *natural state;* and those, which please from some quality, capable of being *illustrated in painting.*"[7] This definition had the salutary effect of teaching generations of English and Americans to appreciate natural beauty with the same attention they would give to a framed canvas, but it contained the seeds of its own satire in suggesting that art might be the prototype of nature, and that visual values could be separated from any others, i.e., moral.

While Gilpin identified certain characteristics of the picturesque (roughness as opposed to beautiful smoothness, ruggedness as opposed to regular delineation, variety and contrast), he also proposed a generalized style of viewing quite at odds with that of the naturalist. "To this it is enough, that the province of the picturesque eye is to *survey nature;* not to *anatomize matter.* It throws its glances around in the broad-cast stile. It comprehends an extensive tract at each sweep. It examines *parts,* but never descends to *particles.*"[8] What Gilpin seems unfortunately to imply is that the tourist may cheerfully ignore detail. And in his recommendation of sketching as a means of remembering the scene later, he goes so far as to advocate improving upon nature if the scene at hand provided too little subject matter. These suggestions later became the object of satirical attack by William Combe and Thomas Rowlandson.

Richard Payne Knight (1750–1824) emphasized the visual nature of the picturesque even more than Gilpin did. In a Note annexed to the second edition of his didactic poem "The Landscape," Knight says "the picturesque is merely that kind of beauty which belongs exclusively to the sense of vision; or to the imagination, guided by that sense."[9] Knight is uncertain whether there even is such a category as the picturesque—but if there is, it pertains to vision only.[10]

Uvedale Price (1747–1829), the third of the major theoreticians on the picturesque, prints Knight's Note in "A Dialogue on the distinct character of the picturesque and the beautiful, in answer to the objections of Mr. Knight." To Knight's and Gilpin's claim that vision is the sense addressed by the picturesque, Price insists on the larger category of perception, a category that includes other senses. He further maintains that the appreciation of the beauty in a hovel, a donkey, or a gypsy is learned, not innate. According to Price, the beautiful has immediate appeal, whereas the picturesque is an acquired taste. Irregularity is adduced by Price as a cause of the picturesque, together with sudden and abrupt deviations.[11]

Essentially, then, the picturesque possessed visual appeal and elicited the cool response, "interesting." Picturesque objects, views, or people did not excite moral or any other concern except the strictly aesthetic. Rough textures, jagged surfaces, irregularity, and variety within the composition were thought particularly picturesque values; the sketch or the ruin was preferred to the complete work; character was preferred to beauty; the artistry of time and accident was stressed.

The picturesque is a momentary, dramatic experience which does not engage the emotions or stir deep thought. A comfortable aesthetic experience, the picturesque tends to make one vaguely aware of his mortality, but not in a manner which threatens one's equanimity. Martin Price captures the essence of the picturesque: "The typical picturesque object or scene—the aged man, the old house, the road with cart-wheel tracks, the irregular village—carries within it the principle of change. All of them imply the passage of time and the slow working of its change upon them."[12]

In the 1830's landscape painting and gardening, town planning, and touring all reflected the mode. "The picturesque became the nineteenth-century's mode of vision," according to Christopher Hussey. "Picturesque scenes and objects appealed to everybody who aspired to the reputation of being 'artistic.' So long as the convention was accepted there was no question of its aesthetic origin or values.

The recognition of the picturesque had become as instinctive as that of day or night."[13]

The painting so much admired by the eighteenth century as to give rise to the picturesque as an aesthetic category was, primarily, that of Claude Lorrain, Gaspar and Nicolas Poussin, and Salvator Rosa, as well as the seventeenth-century Dutch genre and landscape painters. Salvator Rosa's slightly terrifying landscapes with *banditti* or gypsies and ruins of indeterminate age had a particular appeal for the eighteenth and nineteenth-century English, as did the gentler landscapes of Claude Lorrain and Gaspar Poussin with their classic ruins and occasional gods. By Dickens' day appreciation of these painters, whose work was largely done in Italy, and of the seventeenth-century Dutch landscapists had become a mark of genteel connoisseurship even in the middle class. It was in search of such scenes as appeared on these canvases that the English now began to travel.

Guide books proliferated, instructing the Grand Tourist where to go to satisfy his penchant for the picturesque. John Chatwode Eustace's four-volume *Classical Tour through Italy* (1817) was an especially popular continental guide, while William Gilpin helped to establish Britain itself as picturesque touring country. The English spent a small, albeit significant, amount of time traveling in search of the picturesque, but they invested large amounts of time and fortune in transforming their estates and even building whole towns in accordance with picturesque principles. Indeed, that which current travelers find so pleasing in the English countryside is largely the result of eighteenth and nineteenth-century picturesque design.

The landscape values associated with the picturesque appear in some of Dickens' descriptions. In his first novel, *The Pickwick Papers* (1837), Dickens drew a number of gentle picturesque landscapes which contribute to the sense of well-being and contentment which radiate from Mr. Pickwick. Early in the novel Dickens described Rochester, the place of his boyhood which so frequently forms his setting, in a manner which emphasized its picturesqueness:

> On the left of the spectator lay the ruined wall, broken in many places, and in some, overhanging the narrow beach below in rude and heavy masses. Huge knots of sea-weed hung upon the jagged and pointed stones, trembling in every breath of wind; and the green ivy clung mournfully round the dark and ruined battlements. Behind it rose

Salvator Rosa, "Bandits on a Rocky Coast" The Metropolitan Museum of Art. Charles B. Curtis Fund, 1934

Attributed to Claude Lorrain, "Pastoral Landscape" Musée du Louvre

Nicolas Poussin, "Landscape in the Roman Campagna with a man scooping water"
Reproduced by courtesy of the Trustees, The National Gallery, London

> the ancient castle, its towers roofless, and its massive walls crumbling away.... On either side, the banks of the Medway, covered with cornfields and pastures, with here and there a windmill, or a distant church, stretched away as far as the eye could see, presenting a rich and varied landscape, rendered more beautiful by the changing shadows which passed swiftly across it.... as the heavy but picturesque boats glided slowly down the stream.
>
> Ch. V

Here we can see many of the qualities associated with the picturesque: roughness or ruggedness such as that of the "rude and heavy masses," as well as the broken outlines of the "jagged and pointed stones," the "roofless towers," and "crumbling walls;" variety and complexity, as opposed to classical simplicity, here represented by the wide vista with its extensive visual delights; movement, and a sense of transience, suggested by the "skimming clouds" and the flowing river.

It seems highly likely that Dickens, with his many cinematic scenes anticipating film,[14] and with his attraction to the erratic, the unanticipated but telling gesture of a person or movement of a thing, was drawn to the picturesque partly because of the principle of motion inherent in it. In the passage cited above, Dickens places particular emphasis on motion and change in the landscape: "trembling," "crumbling," "changing shadows which passed swiftly," "glided," as he does in other picturesque scenes.

The aspects of the picturesque briefly sketched above carry positive, pleasing connotations, but there was another side to this mode. With its conscious evocation of certain paintings, the picturesque led to excessive imitation and superficiality.

The connoisseur of the picturesque—especially the middle-class connoisseur—made himself an object of ridicule, and indeed had been much ridiculed prior to Dickens' time. Standing with his back to a picturesque scene, oval-shaped Claude glass in hand to reflect the picture back to him, the picturesque traveller could, with some accuracy, be accused of seeing life through a rear-view mirror. Not only did he obtain a second-hand impression through his reflecting glass, but he stood on a spot clearly designated in one of the multiple tour-guides to picturesque scenes, and that scene itself would have been selected because of its resemblance to certain paintings considered picturesque.

There is a certain charm, as well as a good deal of amusement, in watching the picturesque connoisseur during his aesthetic detachment from the earth. But there is also something deeply disturbing in the pleasure he takes from the surface reflection of places he never discovered himself. Uninhabited rural landscapes might be viewed in this second-hand fashion with no harm other than the missed opportunity for probing examination of nature which often reveals something of the self. But urban landscapes viewed in the picturesque manner can have disastrous consequences, for such cursory appraisals dissociate the visual from other human values.

The problem had been noted well before Dickens. Jane Austen chided Henry and Eleanor Tilney in *Northanger Abbey* for admiring only the approved picturesque beauties around Bath. Wordsworth expressed a more serious concern that the picturesque adhered too narrowly to surface details rather than plumbing the depths of one's soul.[15] But in spite of these early warning signals interest in the picturesque lingered on.

Writing in an era when the picturesque affected everyone's vision, Dickens consciously and frequently alluded to the mode. The emphasis on contrasts and on motion, integral elements in the picturesque, had positive appeal for him. But Dickens quickly recognized the dangers inherent in the excessive emphasis on pleasing surface to the exclusion of any moral concerns.

1. PASTORAL PICTURESQUE: *THE PICKWICK PAPERS*

The announced appearance of *The Pickwick Papers* in 1836 implied that it would satirize the picturesque. Dickens' "Advertisement," which appeared just a few days before the opening number, described "Mr. Samuel Pickwick—the great traveller—whose fondness for the useful arts prompted his celebrated journey to Birmingham in the depth of winter, and whose taste for the beauties of nature even led him to penetrate to the very borders of Wales in the height of summer."[16] The satirical thrust at the picturesque traveler is made in two ways: on the one hand by citing the center of industrial ugliness as the goal of a tour, and on the other hand by describing the commonest tour as if it were extraordinary. Dickens continued in the "Advertisement" to explain the activities of Pickwick on his tour. "The whole surface of Middlesex, a part of Surrey, a portion of

Essex, and several square miles of Kent were in their turns examined and reported on." The emphasis on "surface," the painstaking examination of small areas and the expansive reporting of one's observations were all characteristic of the picturesque traveler.

The very people who read Dickens' first novel were likely to take holidays in search of the picturesque. Numerous advertisements in the monthly parts suggest proper destinations, as just a sampling of the titles indicates: *Kidd's New and Picturesque Pocket and Steam-Boat Companion; Finden's Tableaux: or Picturesque Scenes Illustrative of National Character, Beauty, and Costume; Heath's Picturesque Annual* with engravings by Dickens' friend, Daniel Maclise; and *A Series of Views in The Isle of Wight: Embracing Delineations and Descriptions of the Interesting and Picturesque Scenery with which this Garden Island Most Strikingly Abounds.* The latter book is described in extensive Victorian detail: "To the Visitor, this Work, it is presumed, will be found of eminent utility, in facilitating his Tour through this 'Beautiful Island,' and at once acquainting him with the locality of its most romantic and interesting features; whilst, in the mind of the native and resident, it cannot fail of exciting unmingled feelings of delight, as viewing, in 'mimic miniature;' the scenes and objects 'wild and varied,' the originals of which he has so often contemplated with sensations of wonder and admiration."[17]

Within *The Pickwick Papers* Dickens pokes fun at the search for "wild and varied" scenery, and at the lengthy descriptions of it written by countless travelers in search of scenes which resembled paintings. Such satire had precedents, particularly *The Tour of Dr. Syntax in Search of the Picturesque* (1809), in which Thomas Rowlandson and William Combe had satirized William Gilpin's excessively detailed accounts of his British tours. This book, in which Combe's text had been written up to Rowlandson's drawings, clearly served as one of the models for *The Pickwick Papers.*[18] Certainly Robert Seymour must have had that precedent in mind when he suggested to Chapman and Hall that they find a writer to provide the text for a series of prints he proposed.[19] But the brash young Dickens had no intention of playing the secondary role of Combe, and he quickly assumed the direction of the book so that text was primary and illustration followed.[20]

Though he did not emulate the working relationship of Combe and Rowlandson, Dickens does seem to have absorbed some of their methods of satirizing the picturesque. Dr. Syntax, the satirical embodiment of Gilpin, sets out with the note and sketch pads required of the picturesque traveler, determined to find material he can profitably describe:

> I'll make a TOUR—and then I'll WRITE IT.
> You well know what my pen can do,
> And I'll employ my pencil too:—
> I'll ride and *write,* and *sketch* and print,
> And thus create a real mint;
> I'll *prose* it here, I'll *verse* it there,
> And *picturesque* it ev'ry where.

Like his predecessor, Mr. Pickwick sallies forth to seek the picturesque, armed with "his portmanteau in his hand, his telescope in his great-coat pocket, and his notebook in his waistcoat" (Ch. II). The ostensible purpose of Pickwick's travels is to send back reports to the Pickwick Club. Thus the writing of his picturesque adventures is from the outset part of Pickwick's purpose, though this part of Dickens' plan is dropped as the novel proceeds. Satire of amateur scientists and dilettantish archeologists is, of course, also interwoven with satire of the picturesque.

Rowlandson's Dr. Syntax begins his tour confident of finding those "ideal scenes" he knows from landscape painting, but such scenes elude him, and he discovers that if he is not to return empty-handed, he will have to discover the picturesque in the things around him:

> ...as my time shall not be lost,
> I'll make a drawing of the Post;
> And, tho'a flimsy taste may flout it,
> There's something *picturesque* about it:
> 'Tis rude and rough, without a gloss,
> And is well cover'd o'er with moss;

Starting from the simple post, Syntax creates a picturesque landscape complete with "shaggy ridge," water and bridge, all standard features of the picturesque scene. Though he acknowledges that "from truth I haply err," Syntax takes delight in having made "a Landscape of a Post."

Priding himself on finding visual interest where others might see none, the picturesque traveler made himself an object of satire, and Dickens, already in *Sketches by Boz* (1836), had drawn his own version of the type. "Mr. Tomkins was a clerk in a wine-house; he was a connoisseur in paintings, and had a wonderful eye for the picturesque." Standing at his window he inquires of his friend whether he had noted "how splendidly the light falls upon the left side of that broken chimney-pot at No. 48?"

> "Dear me! I see," replied Wisbottle, in a tone of admiration.
>
> "I never saw an object stand out so beautifully against the clear sky in my life," ejaculated Alfred. Everybody...echoed the sentiment; for Mr. Tomkins had a great character for finding out beauties which no one else could discover—he certainly deserved it.

On the page of "The Boarding-House" where this passage appears, Dickens' heading reads, "A Picturesque Object."

This gentle satire appears in the pages of *The Pickwick Papers.* Unlike Combe and Rowlandson, Dickens does not direct his jabs at any one person, but rather at the point of view engendered by the picturesque, at the rather rigid visual expectations and certain accepted verbal responses to them. On Mr. Pickwick's first picturesque adventure, he and his friend Snodgrass make the expected, appropriate responses to the ruin of Rochester Castle, but their traveling companion, the jerky-phrased Jingle, observes the ruin in a manner quite hostile to the picturesque:

> "Magnificent ruin!" said Mr. Augustus Snodgrass, with all the poetic fervour that distinguished him, when they came in sight of the fine old castle.
>
> "What a study for an antiquarian!" were the very words which fell from Mr. Pickwick's mouth, as he applied his telescope to his eye.
>
> "Ah! fine place," said the stranger, "glorious pile—frowning walls—tottering arches—dark nooks—crumbling stair-cases—Old cathedral too—earthy smell—pilgrims' feet worn away the old steps—little Saxon doors—confessionals like money-takers' boxes at theatres—queer customers those monks—Popes, and Lord Treasurers, and all sorts of old fellows, with great red faces, and broken noses, burning up every day—buff jerkins too—match-locks—Sarcophagus—fine place—old legends too—strange stories: capital."
>
> Ch. II

While Snodgrass and Pickwick make superficial, guidebook remarks, Jingle's unschooled responses lead back to the former occupants of the building and introduce all sorts of unpleasant possibilities which make a merely visual experience of the ruin untenable.

Such undercutting of the picturesque manner of viewing a scene occurs throughout the novel, nearly always with humorous intention and effect. Even though certain aspects of the picturesque are exposed to the ridicule of an unsympathetic point of view, the ridicule is held in check. Dickens' intention here is not to level a full-scale attack against the picturesque, but merely to sport with certain of its characteristic features which lent themselves to humorous exaggeration and willful misinterpretation.

Like the ruin, which picturesque connoisseurs found so pleasing, so ivy, which often wound around ruins, softening them and creating interesting surfaces, was thought an inherently picturesque plant. Dickens has a character in *The Pickwick Papers* recite "The Ivy Green," a poem which personifies the plant, creating a macabre impression suggestive of mold and decay rather than a pleasing visual impression:

> Oh, a dainty plant is the Ivy green,
> That creepeth o'er ruins old!
> Of right choice food are his meals I ween,
> In his cell so lone and cold.
> The wall must be crumbled, the stone decayed,
> To pleasure his dainty whim:
> And the mouldering dust that years have made
> Is a merry meal for him.
> Creeping where no life is seen,
> A rare old plant is the Ivy green.
>
> Ch. VI

Ironically, Dickens' mocking poem seems to have appealed to partisans of the picturesque; it was put to music and published separately under a music cover showing the picturesque in its most sentimental, decay-loving guise.[21]

The narrative carries us to a hunt at Dingley Dell where Dickens mocks the notion of viewing human beings as embellishments to landscape. When the hunters are assembled beneath an avenue of trees for rook-shooting, their host suddenly beckons,

> And two ragged boys, who had been marshalled to the spot under the direction of the infant Lambert, forthwith commenced climbing up two of the trees.

> "What are those lads for?" inquired Mr. Pickwick abruptly. He was rather alarmed; for he was not quite certain but that the distress of the agricultural interest, about which he had often heard a great deal, might have compelled the small boys attached to the soil to earn a precarious and hazardous subsistence by making marks of themselves for inexperienced sportsmen.
>
> Ch. VII

The "ragged boys" sent up to beat for birds could be viewed by connoisseurs of the picturesque as ornamental embellishments to the scene. Such was done by George Lambert, named by Hussey "the father of English landscape," who planned his vistas to include such picturesque figures as embellishments. Pickwick's naive question incites our pity, however, and prevents our experiencing the scene merely visually.

On the same grounds where the rook-shooting occurs, there is a garden adorned by a "bower at the further end, with honey-suckle, jessamine, and creeping plants—one of those sweet retreats which humane men erect for the accommodation of spiders" (Ch. VIII). Again Dickens mockingly introduces the unpicturesque point of view, noticing aspects of landscape embellishment which destroy the intended illusion.

Lovers of the picturesque were likely to engage in all sorts of visual distortions in order to see what they wanted to see. A notable instance of this occurs on Captain Boldwig's landscaped grounds. Mr. Pickwick and friends picnic on Boldwig's property, but Pickwick drinks so much cold punch that he cannot accompany his friends on a hunt, electing instead to remain behind sleeping in a wheelbarrow, beneath an oak tree. Both wheelbarrow and oak tree were standard adornments of picturesque landscape,[22] but Pickwick on the scene is obviously a discordant extra. While he slept, "Captain Boldwig, followed by the two gardeners, came striding along as fast as his size and importance would let him; and when he came near the oak tree, Captain Boldwig paused, and drew a long breath, and looked at the prospect as if he thought the prospect ought to be highly gratified at having him to take notice of it; and then he struck the ground emphatically with his stick, and summoned the head-gardener" (Ch. XIX). Not until the gardener points out the fact to him does Boldwig notice the unplanned intrusion on his grounds.

This failure to notice the obvious while cultivating the capacity to admire the picturesque is treated by Dickens in a humorous vein. But towards the end of the novel he touches on an aspect of the picturesque which had serious moral overtones, the encouragement of travelers to see an old village as a pleasing combination of lines and textures while ignoring the poverty therein. Viewing landscape as idealized picture was a relatively harmless activity, albeit one readily satirized. But viewing human habitation as mere picture had the evil consequence of ignoring the human misery often inseparable from the quaint and the old.[23] Late in the novel, at the point where the narrative has taken a darker turn, a traveler walks down the streets of Edinburgh and gains an impression of crowding and decay:

> On either side of him, there shot up against the dark sky, tall gaunt straggling houses, with time-stained fronts, and windows that seemed to have shared the lot of eyes in mortals, and to have grown dim and sunken with age. Six, seven, eight stories high, were the houses; story piled above story, as children build with cards—throwing their dark shadows over the roughly paved road, and making the dark night darker.
>
> Ch. XLIX

Having ascended the hill out of Edinburgh, the traveler pauses to look back, and his visual impression is of a "picturesque old town." Only from a distance does the town have this character; near at hand sordidness overwhelms picturesqueness.

Dickens became increasingly concerned about the proximity of poverty and the picturesque, and sometime later recalled the impression he had gained while accompanying a doctor through "the old town of Edinburgh. In the closes and wynds of that picturesque place—I am sorry to remind you what fast friends picturesqueness and typhus often are—we saw more poverty and sickness in an hour than many people would believe in a life."[24] When Dickens delivered this speech in which poverty and the picturesque are conjoined, he had just completed *Little Dorrit,* a novel which excoriates the evils attendant upon the picturesque point of view. From a humorously satirical treatment of the surface picturesque in his first novel, he had moved to a moral indictment of the picturesque point of view.

2. A CHANGING VIEW

Dickens' use of the picturesque in *Little Dorrit* (1857) is so different from what it was in *The Pickwick Papers* (1837) that one is bound to ask what accounts for the change in view. Morally reprehensible characters with a taste for the picturesque appear in *Nicholas Nickleby* (1839), *Barnaby Rudge* (1841), and *Dombey and Son* (1848), as I explain below. The capacity of landscape to carry varied connotations develops in *Martin Chuzzlewit* where picturesque anticipation of "the Walley of Eden," as Mark Tapley calls it, yields to grotesque reality. But it is the little-read *Pictures from Italy* (1845) that furnishes the most substantive link to *Little Dorrit.* The substantial portion of *Pictures from Italy* is comprised of Dickens' letters to John Forster who remarked that during Dickens' second extended trip in 1853, "his formerly expressed notions as to art and pictures in Italy received confirmation."[25] This later trip must have reinforced the images of the first one and brought them to the forefront of Dickens' consciousness, for many of the observations in *Pictures from Italy* are imaginatively reconstructed in *Little Dorrit.*

Again and again in Italy Dickens found the picturesque accompanied by poverty. "[Genoa] abounds in the strangest contrasts: things that are picturesque, ugly, mean, magnificent, delightful, and offensive, break upon the view at every turn."[26] The charming aspect of Mediterranean towns seen from a distance contrasted sharply with their squalor when seen near at hand. Though the recognition of the relation of the picturesque to poverty had become a commonplace, Dickens found many of his countrymen still exclaiming over the visual delights of wretched dwelling places. From Naples he wrote Forster,

> Oh the miles of miserable streets and wretched occupants, to which Saffron-hill or the Boroughmint is a kind of small gentility, which are found to be so picturesque by English lords and ladies; to whom the wretchedness left behind at home is lowest of the low, and vilest of the vile, and commonest of all common things.[27]

The seemingly inevitable association of poverty with the picturesque led Dickens to suggest as early as 1845 that perhaps a new definition was needed. "I am afraid the conventional idea of the picturesque is associated with such misery and degradation that a new picturesque will have to be established as the world goes onward."[28]

It was not just the poverty concomitant with the picturesque that disturbed Dickens, but the lack of correspondence between the appearance and the reality of a thing. For similar reasons Dickens was irritated during his Italian travels by the pretensions of the artists' models who struck "picturesque attitudes," and waited to be hired as sitters:

> The most aggravating of the party is a dismal old patriarch, with very long white hair and beard, who carries a great staff in his hand.... He is the venerable model. Another man in a sheepskin...is the Pastoral Model. Another man in a brown cloak who leans against a wall with his arms folded, is the assassin model....they are one and all the falsest rascals in Rome or out of it: being specially made up for their trade, and having no likeness among the whole population.[29]

Dickens was concerned that people would take a man's costume for his substance, in the same manner they judged a village by its outer appearance. Further, while artists were painting these characters dressed to appear picturesque, they were neglecting to paint real people in actual circumstances. To Miss Coutts he recalled having seen in paintings at the Royal Academy just such poses as those struck by the Italian models, and it was this that led him to deride the "Fine Arts" as being more concerned with waxwork than with reality.[30]

While Dickens was collecting these visual impressions of the picturesque and its associations, he was also becoming more aware of the incipient perniciousness in the picturesque as a point of view. There are a number of characters in his novels who profess themselves to be connoisseurs of the picturesque, and they are an increasingly sinister lot. The first of these, Mrs. Nickleby (1839), shares some humorous similarities with Pickwickian characters, but she also is the willing, though unwitting, collaborator in a scheme which might have ruined her daughter. Because of her pretensions to grandeur and romance she fails to see important aspects of reality around her. Seeking to impress Mr. Pluck and Mr. Pyke, two borderline members of the upper class interested in Kate, Mrs. Nickleby "went on to entertain her guests with a lament over her fallen fortunes, and a picturesque account of her old house in the country; comprising a full description of the different apartments" (Ch. XXVII).

Associating the picturesque with Mrs. Nickleby seems harmless enough, but seen in the full context of Dickens' work she emerges as the earliest of many increasingly reprehensible characters whose visual taste reflects a shallowness of moral perception. Sir John Chester, the dilettantish, unacknowledged father of Hugh in *Barnaby Rudge* (1841), surveys the ruins of the Haredale house where his own relatives once lived. "'How very picturesque this is!'—he pointed, as he spoke, to the dismantled house, and raised his glass to his eye" (Ch. LXXXI). In fact the mansion ruins are accurately described, but it is one thing for Dickens to draw a picturesque impression of the ruin and quite another for Chester, standing as if in a gallery, to attach this epithet. Not only does the term suggest a cold distance from the human tragedy, but Chester himself is responsible for the fire, having sent others to burn out his enemies. He stands surveying his own picturesque creation, as it were. The result of Dickens' placing him in such a situation and giving him such a line is a final devastation of character, the ultimate proof that he is utterly dissolute.

Similar use of visual taste to reveal moral poverty occurs in *Dombey and Son* (1848) where Mrs. Skewton holds forth on the picturesque. Her comments are fuller and more revealing of her own character than is true of characters in the earlier novels. Mrs. Skewton, rather like her predecessor Mrs. Nickleby, is so desirous of her daughter's marrying well that she is willing to sacrifice her daughter's happiness in order to gain this dubious goal. Predictably, her interest in the picturesque reflects her moral vacuity. To Mr. Carker she waxes eloquent on the Middle Ages. "'Such charming times!' cried Cleopatra. 'So full of faith! So vigorous and forcible! So picturesque! So perfectly removed from commonplace'" (Ch. XXVII). She returns to the subject a few pages later. "'Those darling bygone times, Mr. Carker,' said Cleopatra, 'with their delicious fortresses, and their dear old dungeons, and their delightful places of torture, and their romantic vengeances, and their picturesque assaults and sieges, and everything that makes life truly charming! How dreadfully we have degenerated!'" (Ch. XXVII). Mrs. Skewton's impression of the past is a pastiche of the romantic picturesque, even in her revealingly sadistic selection of medieval tortures. Her habit of viewing the world as picture is consonant with her adoption of Cleopatra as her own image—all is, of course, far from reality.

While Dickens was observing the contiguity of poverty and the picturesque, and castigating admirers of this visual mode, he was also acquiring a deeper pessimism about the future of his country. As the idea for *Little Dorrit* was taking form he wrote Forster,

> ...a country which is discovered to be in this tremendous condition as to its war affairs; with an enormous black cloud of poverty in every town which is spreading and deepening every hour, and not one man in two thousand knowing anything about, or even believing in, its existence; with a non-working aristocracy, and a silent parliament, and everybody for himself and *nobody for the rest;* this is the prospect, and I think it a very deplorable one.[31]

The original title for the book Dickens began writing a month after this letter was "Nobody's Fault."[32] In this book he brought together his gloom over the inadequacy of British institutions and his feeling that the picturesque point of view was morally hollow. Dickens laid the responsibility for what had gone wrong in English society upon no one in particular, nor upon any single institution, but upon the point of view which tainted them all, a view analogous to the picturesque.

3. THE PICTURESQUE PLAGUE: *LITTLE DORRIT*

Imprisonment sounds the keynote at the beginning of *Little Dorrit* so forcefully as to become metaphor. The characters, yearning for access to the outer world, establish an image of separation from reality that is repeatedly emphasized throughout the novel. But this removal from reality comes to be recognized more as a psychic than a physical phenomenon. And Dickens' method makes clear to us that true perception of reality is a rarity—in the world of the novel or in the world we inhabit.

What is cultivated instead is a surface pleasantry that masks reality—be it the surface of a face, a portrait, or a dwelling—or be it that pursuit of picturesque pleasantry known as the Grand Tour. Although the most affluent members of society are best able to indulge their taste for soul-constricting art and travel, the attitude that prefers surface to substance pervades all levels of society like a plague.

This attitude might be called the picturesque point of view, an attitude that encourages delight in surface, that intentionally separates the visual from the moral experience, that devotes its fullest energy to resembling a work of art from the past. The essentially derivative nature of the picturesque can also make it deceptive and delusory, as we see in *Little Dorrit.*

The frontispiece, "Fanny and Little Dorrit Call on Mrs. Merdle," shows us the entrance to the Merdle Mansion, home of the wealthiest character in the book. By conscious or unconscious design—it little matters which—the footman in the foreground mimics the stance and gesture of the neoclassical sculpture just behind him. Pretentiousness, pomposity, and a fraudulent presentation both of self and of the Merdle household are captured in that picturesque imitation.

At the opposite end of the social scale is Mrs. Plornish of Bleeding-Heart Yard who indulges a picturesque fantasy by having her shop "painted to represent the exterior of a thatched cottage.... No Poetry and no Art ever charmed the imagination more than the union of the two in this counterfeit cottage charmed Mrs. Plornish.... To Mrs. Plornish, it was still a most beautiful cottage, a most wonderful deception" (Bk. II, Ch. 13). The chapter in which the Happy Cottage appears is titled "The Progress of an Epidemic" and Dickens speaks at the outset about the difficulty of curbing a moral infection. Even the lowly Plornish family has been caught up in the general mania to live with fictions rather than reality.

That rich and poor should be infected by the same aesthetic disease should not surprise us in a book carefully structured into two parts entitled "Poverty" and "Riches." The opening chapter, "Sun and Shadow," presents us with fundamental contrasts, and the two initial plates do the same. The frontispiece contrasts with the title page showing Little Dorrit stepping out of the prison. She is dressed exactly the same in each, and is shown to us from the same perspective. Yet she steps indoors into opulence in one, outdoors from poverty in the other. Using Little Dorrit as an observer, the novel shows us how intimately related are those two worlds seemingly so separate. When her fortunes rise and she makes the Grand Tour with her family, Little Dorrit cannot reconcile the dream-like fantasy of the present with the remembered reality of the past:

> All that she saw was new and wonderful, but it was not real; it seemed to her as if those visions of mountains and picturesque countries

> might melt away at any moment, and the carriage, turning some abrupt corner, bring up with a jolt at the old Marshalsea gate.... Among the day's unrealities would be...white villages and towns on hillsides, lovely without, but frightful in their dirt and poverty within...beggars of all sorts everywhere: pitiful, picturesque, hungry, merry: children beggars and aged beggars.
>
> Bk. II, Ch. 3

But Little Dorrit is the only member of her entourage who sees the essential unreality of the picturesque, just as she is the only one who recognizes similarities between the prisoners she once knew and the tourists she now encounters:

> It appeared on the whole, to Little Dorrit...that this same society in which they lived, greatly resembled a superior sort of Marshalsea. Numbers of people seemed to come abroad, pretty much as people had come into the prison; through debt, through idleness, relationship, curiosity, and general unfitness for getting on at home.... They prowled about the churches and picture-galleries, much in the old, dreary, prison-yard manner.... A certain set of words and phrases, as much belonging to tourists as the College and the Snuggery belonged to the jail, was always in their mouths.
>
> Bk. II, Ch. 7

This is a society all of a piece, as in *Bleak House,* and affected, similarly, by a widespread contagion. Whether physically incarcerated or not, the characters here are constricted by social convention and prevented from perceiving reality by their absorption in surface appearance.

That cultivation of surface is directly connected to the commercial activity of this society, the acquiring of money. Pancks, rent-collector for the picturesquely patriarchal figure of Casby, tells Arthur Clennam that a man is made for business. "Keep me always at it, and I'll keep you always at it, you keep somebody else always at it. There you are with the Whole Duty of Man in a commercial country" (Bk. I, Ch. 13). A perverted, even blasphemous "Whole Duty of Man," yet one which oddly accords with a form of Christianity the Puritannical repression of which affords room for shrewd financial dealings.

At the top of the social scale Mr. Merdle, in spite of his ignominious name, enjoys the prominence and esteem once accorded royalty—all because he has amassed more money than anyone else.

> All people knew (or thought they knew) that he had made himself immensely rich; and, for that reason alone, prostrated themselves before him, more degradedly and less excusably than the darkest savage creeps out of his hole in the ground to propitiate, in some log or reptile, the Deity of his benighted soul.
>
> Bk. II, Ch. 12

And this social obeisance continues for a man whose physical bearing suggests a character deserving something less than worship.

> There was a spectre always attendant on him, saying... "Are such the signs you trust, and love to honour; this head, these eyes, this mode of speech, the tone and manner of this man?"...rather ugly questions these, always going about town with Mr. Merdle; and there was a tacit agreement that they must be stifled.
>
> Bk. II, Ch. 12

Society refuses to question, until it is too late, its own uneasiness at granting such a man such esteem. Indeed, this society so infatuated with money does not like to admit its indiscretion. Money must be pursued—but the pursuer must not admit it. Gentility requires the preservation of the fiction that something other than money is the driving concern. Here, too, this infectious fiction runs from top to bottom of society. In the debtors' prison Mr. Dorrit preserves the genteel fiction of receiving "testimonials" rather than out-right handouts; Mr. Merdle, who would seem to *be* Society, finds he is still under the necessity of conforming to Society's surface requirements.

Merdle's wife sweetly tells him, "If you wish to know the complaint I make against you, it is, in so many plain words, that you really ought not to go into Society unless you can accommodate yourself to Society." And since he is at a loss to know just how he has failed to accommodate himself, she spells it out for him. "I don't expect you...to captivate people. I don't want you to take any trouble upon yourself, or to try to be fascinating. I simply request you to care about nothing—or seem to care about nothing—as everybody else does" (Bk. I, Ch. 33).

"Everybody else" includes, principally, the Barnacles encrusted in the Circumlocution Office and in all the other realms of officialdom. Mr. Tite Barnacle, for instance, "was altogether splendid, massive, over-powering, and impracticable. He seemed to have been sitting for his portrait to Sir Thomas Lawrence all the days of his life" (Bk. I, Ch. 10). The fancy portrait, as painted by Lawrence and his ilk, was designed to look impressive, and, as Dickens saw, deceptive. Bits of costume were made to pass for indications of character. Buttons, for instance, "It is certain that the man to whom importance is accorded is the buttoned-up man. Mr. Tite Barnacle never would have passed for half his current value, unless his coat had been always buttoned-up to his white cravat" (Bk. II, Ch. 12).

Dickens pokes splendid satirical fun at these stuffed dummies by placing them as figures in a painting by Cuyp, a seventeenth-century Dutch landscapist whose work was approvedly picturesque. "[Mr. Tite Barnacle] and Mr. Merdle, seated diverse ways and with ruminating aspects on a yellow ottoman in the light of the fire, holding no verbal communication with each other, bore a strong general resemblance to the two cows in the Cuyp picture over against them." Two paragraphs later Dickens has the pompous Lord Decimus Barnacle arrive. "His Lordship composed himself into the picture after Cuyp, and made a third cow in the group" (Bk. II, Ch. 12). Aspiring to picturesque coolness, to impenetrable expressions that betray no emotion whatever, these modern moguls have succeeded in forming themselves after the picturesque model they have so sedulously studied, and they now resemble that most picturesque of creatures, the cow.

In this society which commends the impassive, even bovine surface, the bare suggestion of genuine curiosity is stifled. "This right little, tight little island" (Bk. I, Ch. 6) will not admit the probing question. Clennam creates consternation in the Circumlocution Office merely by demanding, "I want to know." Little Dorrit betrays her lack of gentility by expressing a sense of wonder in Venice. She is sharply reprimanded by Mrs. General, the professional shaper of demeanor, and told "It is better not to wonder." Rather be blasé, uninterested, never showing what one really feels—and, eventually, perhaps, arriving at that miraculous social state of feeling nothing at all.

One may give the appearance of feeling, but only the vulgar actually betray genuine emotion. It is a society made for dissemblers, and we get several masters of the art, always presented to us with reference to the picturesque. The first character we meet is a melodramatic villain capable of transforming his features into those of a gentleman. Rigaud-Blandois "had a certain air of being a handsome man—which he was not. It was mere swagger and challenge; but in this particular, as in many others, blustering assertion goes for proof, half over the world" (Bk. I, Ch. 1).

Blandois parleys into the means of an uncertain livelihood that theatrical ability to resemble a gentleman. He readily identifies with the picturesque, a quality which he recognizes in the Clennam house. "An old house is a weakness with me. I have many weaknesses, but none greater. I love and study the picturesque in all its varieties. I have been called picturesque myself. It is no merit to be picturesque—I have greater merits, perhaps—but I may be, by an accident" (Bk. I, Ch. 30). Blandois has the strongly-marked facial features and the dashing costume typical of Salvator Rosa's outlaw, and he seems, by reputation and behavior, capable of acting like what he appears. But he never really does anything. He remains bluster and swagger, though capable of inspiring fear.

Later in the novel Blandois is taken up and used as a model by the dilettante artist, Henry Gowan:

> He found a pleasure in setting up Blandois as the type of elegance, and making him a satire upon others who piqued themselves on personal graces. He seriously protested that the bow of Blandois was perfect, that the address of Blandois was irresistible, and that the picturesque ease of Blandois would be cheaply purchased (if it were not a gift, and unpurchaseable) for a hundred thousand francs.
>
> Bk. II, Ch. 6

Blandois' "picturesque ease" means he can serve as a model for a villain or a gentleman—with the result that we question whether there is much difference in these characters.

When Little Dorrit and company visit Gowan's studio, they first see "Blandois of Paris in a great cloak and a furtive slouched hat, standing on a throne platform in a corner," and Little Dorrit instinctively recoils from him. Yet Gowan insists that his model may represent "A bravo waiting for his prey, a distinguished noble waiting to save his country, the common enemy waiting to do somebody a bad turn, an angelic messenger waiting to do somebody a good turn—whatever you think he looks most like" (Bk. II, Ch. 6). Blandly asserting the possibility of the most divergent interpretations, Gowan disavows any artistic responsibility for representing accurately what he sees. He means only to please by catering to shallow taste, but both Little Dorrit and Gowan's dog Lion recognize a potential for evil in the artist's model. Little Dorrit expresses a subdued repugnance, but Lion lunges fiercely towards Blandois in a scene illustrated by Phiz captioned "Instinct Stronger than Training." This tension between "Instinct" and "Training" operates throughout the novel, with the clear suggestion that Training, especially that supplied through the arts, has simply confused accurate perception.

At the opposite end of the social scale, Christopher Casby manages to con the public for years solely by cultivating a benign appearance. We first see Casby through his childish portrait painted in the manner of Lawrence. In one of those spurious situations contrived by such portraitists he is shown "with a haymaking rake, for which he had had, at any time, as much taste or use as for a diving-bell; and sitting...upon a bank of violets, moved to precocious contemplation by the spire of a village church" (Bk. I, Ch. 13). From the smooth-faced boy sitting within an unreal environment, Casby the man has changed very little, only growing his hair long and causing himself to look benevolent. Because of his appearance he is called a patriarch, even the Last of the Patriarchs:

> So grey, so slow, so quiet, so impassionate, so very bumpy in the head, Patriarch was the word for him. He had been accosted in the streets, and respectfully solicited to become a patriarch for painters and for sculptors; with so much importunity, in sooth, that it would appear to be beyond the Fine Arts to remember the points of a Patriarch or to invent one.
>
> Bk. I, Ch. 13

Casby's surface benignity masks his cunning and enables him to extort high rents from the poor.

> It was said that his being town-agent to Lord Decimus Tite Barnacle was referable, not to his having the least business capacity, but to his looking so supremely benignant that nobody could suppose the property screwed or jobbed under such a man.... In a word, it was represented...that many people select their models, much as the painters...select theirs; and that, whereas in the Royal Academy some evil old ruffian of a Dog-stealer will annually be found embodying all the cardinal virtues, on account of his eyelashes, or his chin, or his legs (thereby planting thorns of confusion in the breasts

> of the more observant students of nature), so, in the great social Exhibition, accessories are often accepted in lieu of the internal character.
>
> Bk. I, Ch. 13

Dickens has integrated his observations on artists' models in *Pictures from Italy* into an exposure of the interlocked aesthetics and ethics of his time. What prevents any fundamental reform of social inequities is not a single Casby, Merdle or even the Barnacles' Circumlocution Office. The obstacle to change is, rather, the moral failure to recognize that evil may wear a pleasing mask, and the related aesthetic failure to distinguish between painted fictions, be they portraits or people, canvas or "natural" landscapes, and reality.

Just as composed faces or painted portraits may mask reality, so may houses in this novel. Dickens draws meaning not only from the presented surface, but from the tension between what is seen and what is concealed. The Clennam house has picturesque qualities which identify it more with the sublime than the beautiful. Dark, shadowy, funereal furnishings are seen only obscurely, and the effect is to inspire fear. The decor of the house, as well as its occupants, leans toward the grotesque generally, and toward the Egyptian Revival specifically. During this period of eclecticism the Egyptian style was particularly popular in cemeteries, and Dickens has merely transferred these associations to the Clennam House and inhabitants. Pictures like the "Plagues of Egypt" grace the mausoleum-like interior, while Mrs. Clennam is repeatedly described as being "cold and like a statue." A living mummy she is, but the Dickens of 1855 lets slip the opportunity for a bad pun.

Blandois, lover of the picturesque, is closely linked to this house, both by his own remark and by two plates drawn by Phiz: "Mr. Flintwinch has a mild attack of irritability" and "Damocles." The house becomes an important visual symbol of the moral shoddiness engendered by the picturesque. "It is a genuine old house," Mrs. Clennam tells Blandois, but it becomes apparent that the age of the house is its only genuine feature. Propped up by huge buttresses to prevent its tumbling into the street, this old house shelters people whose moral foundations also require external reinforcement. Mrs. Clennam for years has lived the severe life of self-denial urged by doctrinaire Protestants, yet her demeanor of rigid propriety conceals a heart full of deception. She has simultaneously denied Arthur the true knowledge of his birth, and Little Dorrit access to wealth belonging to her.

The Meagles house, set in the country and conveying an idyllic air, seems the very antithesis of the Clennam ruin set in the squalor and social chaos of London. But the charming Meagles cottage is closely related to the Clennam house, and not only because the house so clearly reflects the nature of the inhabitants. The Meagles house is at the other end of the picturesque spectrum, offering visual pleasure inclining toward the beautiful rather than the grotesque sublime, but appearances mask reality here as much as in the Clennam house:

> [The Meagles house] stood in a garden, no doubt as fresh and beautiful in the May of the Year, as Pet now was in the May of her life; and it was defended by a goodly show of handsome trees and spreading evergreens, as Pet was by Mr. and Mrs. Meagles. It was made out of an old brick house, of which a part had been altogether pulled down, and another part had been changed into the present cottage; so there was a hale elderly portion, to represent Mr. and Mrs. Meagles, and a young, picturesque, very pretty portion to represent Pet.
>
> Bk. I, Ch. 16

This is all very charming and visually pleasing, but, seen in light of the ensuing events of Pet's life, something is obviously lacking in the country cottage, as it has been lacking in her upbringing. Pet cannot forever be "defended" by the "goodly show" of her doting parents, and they, absorbed in their pursuit of the picturesque, have not prepared her to face life on her own where she will have to distinguish between pleasing surfaces and hollow substance. They have taken their pretty daughter to see the world, but they have not taught her to plumb its depths; they have surrounded her with charming things, but they have not taught her to understand herself or other people.

The exterior of the house suggests some of this; the interior with its "vast miscellany" of *objets d'art* "collected on...various expeditions" is even more indicative of the fundamental imperception in the Meagles parents. "There were antiquities from Central Italy, made by the best modern houses in that department of industry;" and scores of tourist trappings obviously acquired while making the Grand Tour.

> There were views, like and unlike, of a multitude of places; and there was one little picture-room devoted to a few of the regular sticky old Saints, with sinews like whipcord, hair like Neptune's, wrinkles like tattooing, and such coats of varnish that every holy personage served for a fly-trap, and became what is now called in the vulgar tongue a Catch-em-alive O.

Meagles thinks of these things as his "spoils" and has no original insights about any of them, nor any particular interest in them. He has only done and acquired what was expected of the picturesque traveler. "Of these pictorial acquisitions Mr. Meagles spoke in the usual manner. He was no judge, he said, except of what pleased himself; he had picked them up, dirt-cheap, and people *had* considered them rather fine" (Bk. I, Ch. 16). Meagles has depended on guidebooks and on others who he assumes understand art to tell him of his collection's worth, to assure him that he has a Guercino, and perhaps a Sebastiano del Piombo.

Meagles' interest in the surface picturesque is bound up with other aspects of his character. He is connected with the Circumlocution Office, that bureaucratic nightmare which functions on the principle of How Not to Do it. After visiting Meagles with Daniel Doyce, Arthur Clennam muses "whether there might be in the breast of this honest, affectionate, and cordial Mr. Meagles, any microscopic portion of the mustard-seed that had sprung up into the great tree of the Circumlocution Office" (Bk. I, Ch. 16). What sets Clennam to pondering this way is his perception that Meagles feels superior to Doyce because the latter is "an originator and a man out of the beaten track of other men" (Bk. I, Ch. 16). Meagles neither understands nor trusts genuinely creative people, for his own professional life has proceeded in bureaucratic channels, as his visual taste has been guided by experts.

Another feature of Meagles' character, closely intertwined with his role as a bureaucrat and pursuer of the picturesque, is his tendency to see people as surfaces only. The tendency is shown in his response to the mercurial behavior of Tattycoram: "Count five-and-twenty, Tattycoram," he responds mechanically to this distraught foundling he has brought into his home. Other members of his household are treated as surface embellishments—two parlormaids, for instance, "who were a highly ornamental part of the table decoration" (Bk. I, Ch. 16).

The results of growing up in this household, so genial but so shallow, can be seen in Pet. Her first independent decision, the choice of a marriage partner, is disastrous. She cannot see, until it is too late, the solidity and strength of character in the older, more reserved Arthur Clennam, but chooses instead the handsome, hollow young artist, Henry Gowan. She elects picture over substance, and the effect of this choice on her life is vividly seen in the change in her dwelling:

> The house, on a little desert island, looked as if it had broken away from somewhere else, and had floated by chance into its present anchorage, in company with a vine almost as much in want of training as the poor wretches who were lying under its leaves. The features of the surrounding picture were, a church with boarding and scaffolding about it...a number of houses at odds with one another and grotesquely out of the perpendicular, like rotten pre-adamite cheeses cut into fantastic shapes and full of mites.
>
> Bk. II, Ch. 6

On the bottom floor of the Gowan house the windows are barred, giving the place the appearance of a prison.

Both of Pet's homes are picturesque, but in quite different ways. Her childhood cottage suggests the Gothic revival at its best, while the bridal bower leans toward the morbid, grotesque side of the picturesque. Variety and motion there are, but thrown together in such a manner as to suggest frenzy rather than control, festering decay rather than gentle ruin. As a picture of Pet's married life, the island house connotes a diminution of security and support, as does the crumbling scaffolding around the old church. Gowan has not proved to be a supportive husband economically or in any other way.

Viewed by tourists, Pet's island home undoubtedly had picturesque appeal, just as her position as an artist's wife seemed idyllic to the obtuse observer. Fanny Dorrit, one of the least perceptive characters of the book, imagines that Pet lives picturesquely: "Love in a cottage, painting pictures for dinner, was so delightfully interesting"[33] (Bk. II, Ch. 6).

Henry Gowan is the suitable artist for this shallow society, and a pivotal figure in the novel. Dickens himself saw Gowan as an integral part of his pattern. "Society, the Circumlocution Office, and Mr. Gowan, are of course three parts of one idea and design, " Dickens wrote Forster.[34]

Gowan not only comes from the upper classes, but he makes his living by painting them and catering to their taste for the picturesque. He would have preferred to have a living provided for him by the Barnacles, whose control of the Circumlocution Office provided plenty of nondemanding bureaucratic jobs, but that was not to be:

> At last he had declared that he would become a Painter; partly because he had always had an idle knack that way, and partly to grieve the souls of the Barnacles-in-chief who had not provided for him. So it had come to pass successively, first, that several distinguished ladies had been frightfully shocked; then, that portfolios of his performances had been handed about o'nights, and declared with ecstasy to be perfect Claudes, perfect Cuyps, perfect phaenomena.
> Bk. I, Ch. 17

Gowan sees himself as an imposter (Bk. I, Ch. 26); he cynically masters the knack of picturesque painting in order to sell pictures and dismisses as so much "hocus-pocus" Clennam's talk of devotion to a vocation (Bk. I, Ch. 34).

Gowan, whose talent is compared to Claude's and Cuyp's, turns to portrait painting as a means of making a living. The meretricious quality of Gowan's portraits reflects the same phoniness Dickens attacks in the picturesque. Incapable of rendering his subjects accurately (Little Dorrit remarks of her father's portrait that "I am not quite convinced I should have known from the likeness if I had not seen him doing it" [Bk. II, Ch. 11]), Gowan trades on flattery and deception. He is only too willing to cater to the demands of the Grand Tourist, like the newly-affluent Dorrit. Undisciplined, lacking in professional commitment, Gowan paints picturesque productions which are consciously shallow, allowing for any interpretation the viewer wishes to attach to them.

Just as Gowan paints the false and shallow face of this society, so Mrs. General shapes the face that is presented. Her role in this society so uncertain of its direction and so out of touch with its own being is to provide people with the proper received responses and expressions. It is a critical indication of the essentially derivative nature of this society that even one's words must be those approved by someone else. It is, in short, an extension of the picturesque point of view formed by guide-book writers like Eustace, on whom Dickens lavished contempt:

> The whole body of travellers seemed to be a collection of voluntary human sacrifices, bound hand and foot, and delivered over to Mr. Eustace and his attendants, to have the entrails of their intellects arranged according to the taste of that sacred priesthood...hosts of tongue-tied and blindfolded moderns were carefully feeling their way, incessantly repeating Prunes and Prism, in the endeavor to set their lips according to the received form.... Nobody had an opinion. There was a formation of surface going on...on an amazing scale, and it had not a flaw of courage or honest free speech in it.
>
> Bk. II, Ch. 7[35]

The "formed" surface resulting from over-exposure to the picturesque is a bland one, carefully avoiding any moral dimension and observing only the visually enticing. In Mrs. General's words, "A truly refined mind will seem to be ignorant of the existence of anything that is not perfectly proper, placid, and pleasant" (Bk. II, Ch. 5).

Anything not fitting these bland categories Mrs. General varnishes over, seeking to dissemble any unpleasantness out of existence, just as contemporary painters sought through varnish to make their work resemble that of old masters. But, of course, this fantasy cannot hold, not with gallons of varnish. Reality, in the form of the grotesque, intrudes into this picturesque world.

Disaster is implicit in the initial contrasts established early in the book and in the first two plates. It is further forecast by the scene in the Alps at the beginning of Book Two where a standard picturesque scene suddenly turns to a grotesque vision of ruins, failed vegetation, and "blackened skeleton arms of wood" as darkness falls.

As reality intrudes at the end of the book, Mr. Merdle moves toward his suicide in a posture oddly evocative of the Dance of Death. "Mr. Merdle, in going down the street, appear[s] to leap, and waltz, and gyrate, as if he were possessed of several Devils" (Bk. II, Ch. 24). Christopher Casby, the picturesque Patriarch, with a pass of Pancks' shears, becomes a grotesque: "a bare-polled, goggle-eyed, big-headed lumbering personage...not in the least venerable" (Bk. II, Ch. 32). And Blandois perishes unexpectedly as the picturesque Clennam house literally falls apart.[36] Thus does grotesque reality rush in to make an end of an unreal, picturesque society.

What we see at the end are Arthur and Little Dorrit "married, with the sun shining on them through the painted figure of Our Saviour on the window" (Bk. II, Ch. 34). That beneficent image behind them, these two sober realists walk down "into the roaring streets," into pulsing life with all its noise and disorder, with all its unrelieved contrasts. The varnished, false pretenses of the picturesque are left in the ruins of the commercial apparatus it helped to sustain. But there is no genuine exuberance at the demise of the picturesque and all it connoted, for the defeat is but partial. And the reality, as Dickens well knew, was that the picturesque would continue to exercise its fantastic hold for many years to come.

Chapter Two
The Grotesque Realism of Hogarth

PETER CONRAD rightly says that "Dickens is the least picturesque of the Victorians, and thus the truest to the rowdy, grotesque, chaotic life of London."[1] Distrustful of the picturesque, Dickens tried to instill similar distrust in his readers so they would not accept false images of reality. What they might overlook was the reality of London to which Conrad alludes, and to assist his readers in *seeing* this reality, Dickens employed the grotesque.

With grotesque imagery Dickens leads us behind varnished and placid surfaces into a world of tumultuous realities unacknowledged by the picturesque. Distortions to the point of ugliness meet our amazed eyes, but the eye cannot linger long over these kinesthetic images that pulse, leap, and cavort across the page. Grotesque imagery assaults the eye, takes the breath away, and leads us to see, really to see, aspects of reality hitherto obscured.

Twentieth-century readers have less difficulty accepting the grotesque as an aesthetic category than the picturesque, for, as Wolfgang Kayser puts it, "The art of our own day shows a greater affinity to the grotesque than that of any other epoch,"[2] while the picturesque is no longer operative. Kayser, still the most authoritative scholar of the grotesque, has traced the origins of the term back to fifteenth-century discoveries of Roman grotto art, and has described some of its distinctive features especially as they appear in German literature. Because of his national concentration, he makes some judgments that are not quite accurate, as when he says that the Victorian age in England "was hardly favorable to such tendencies [as the grotesque]"[3] and then goes on to plead no time for investigating Dickens, whose grotesquerie he admits. Arthur Clayborough offers a corrective to Kayser's view by reminding us of the numerous Victorians who wrote on and about the grotesque: Walter Bagehot, John Ruskin, Robert Browning, John Addington Symonds.[4]

In spite of his restricted investigation, Kayser's working definition of the grotesque furnishes a good starting point. "The grotesque world is—and is not, our own world. The ambiguous way in which we are affected by it results from our awareness that the familiar and apparently harmonious world is alienated under the impact of abysmal forces, which break it up and shatter its coherence."[5] The grotesque elicits fear, for the transformation of our world occurs with such suddenness and surprise that one no longer has the assurance of stability, continuity, and order. Monsters range through the grotesque, weird combinations of vegetable, animal, and human forms that do not occur in nature. Tools and objects are likely to "unfold a dangerous life of their own."[6] The animate and the inanimate, categories we might innocently have considered fixed, suddenly interchange.

Arthur Clayborough questions whether Kayser's criterion of suddenness is so significant.[7] Some works, he rightly points out, are grotesque from the outset; *Hard Times* might be cited as one. Furthermore, while Kayser says we fear the grotesque because we would not want to live in such a world, Clayborough, grounding his investigation in Freud and Jung, points out that we are both repelled and fascinated by the grotesque.[8] Clayborough cites Santayana's definition of the grotesque as "the suggestively monstrous"[9] and also offers an apt definition of his own. "In general, it may be said that the chief idea involved in the various senses of the term grotesque is that of incongruity, of a conflict between some phenomenon and an existing conception of what is natural, fitting, etc."[10] This latter definition is most useful for the following discussion of Dickens' grotesque.

The world of the grotesque has been painted by Hieronymus Bosch, Pieter Breughel the Elder, Francisco Goya and Jacques Callot, and, in our century, by James Ensor, Max Ernst, and Salvador Dali, among others. The Dance of Death, wherein human beings confront a grisly skeletal figure, is an off-shoot of the grotesque with obscure origins in the middle ages, and with continuing manifestations in our own time.

The grotesque would seem to be an enduring phenomenon, though its particular forms may vary with the period. Ruskin recognized that "the grotesque [is] not only a most forceful instrument of teaching, but a most natural manner of expression, springing as it does at once from any tendency to playfulness in minds highly comprehensive of truth."[11]

In the nineteenth century, with its aesthetic so shaped by the picturesque, the grotesque operated as a kind of polar opposite. A narrow line separates the picturesque from the grotesque. Frequently what distinguishes one mode from the other is the perception of the observer, or the angle from which the scene is observed. Pet Meagles' wedding bower, for instance, appears grotesquely mite-ridden and precarious to Dickens as narrator-observer; but to the obtuse Fanny Dorrit it is the picturesque scene of "Love in a cottage." Even a shadow passing over the sun rapidly transforms a scene of picturesque alpine beauty into a terrifying landscape full of grotesque possibility, as we see in *Little Dorrit.*

The grotesque inverts the picturesque. What seemed pleasing variety in the one becomes unsettling chaos in the other. What evoked picture now evokes nightmare, and, indeed, the grotesque was sometimes called *"sogni dei pittori,"* or dreams of the painters.[12] A sense of gentle motion either rigidifies into a condition of stasis or accelerates into random, erratic movement. Marks indicative of mellowing age now turn to signs of outright decrepitude. The same technique of juxtaposition produces in the picturesque an interesting congruence, while in the grotesque juxtaposition results in jarring discrepancy. The picturesque delight in texture turns to a grotesque emphasis on decay. The facial lines indicative of character now result in distortion or grimace. What was intended to please now is destined to startle. Dickens perceived an intimate connection between these two opposite modes, and he used them repeatedly, in conjunction or separately, to satirize the underlying attitudes of his age.

William Hogarth (1697–1764) was one who taught Dickens how to show visually that a pleasing appearance could mask a quite different reality. Often Hogarth suggests that disparity between appearance and reality by means of the grotesque. He imbues inanimate objects with motion; he gives the human physiognomy a bestial look; he draws animals mimicing human beings. Hogarth's is a world in which the conventional, expected order ceases—a world, therefore, of frightening and unanticipated possibility.

In his "modern moral subjects" Hogarth sought to show what happened to the human character as a result of immoral or unfeeling acts. Through physiognomy and through gesture Hogarth revealed the distortions of character accompanying immoral deeds or unavoidable poverty. Often those disfigurements wrought by sin or disease are so markedly inhuman as to become grotesque. In addition to the characters, Hogarth made setting and ancillary detail also "tell" on the scene, often with grotesque implications. Pictures, for instance, instead of just hanging quietly on the walls, seem to participate vigorously in the action; buildings, instead of presenting a stolid, immovable presence, seem often caught at the moment of collapse. Hogarth's is a world in motion, in transition, where the turbulence of passion and intrigue erupts behind the placid facade.

Although his medium is verbal, and his concern psychological, Dickens learned from Hogarth that moral choice is no mere abstraction; it leaves visible consequences. Hogarth's "modern moral subjects" paved the way for Dickens' treatment of street life and served him as classical mythology did earlier writers. Assuming his readers' familiarity with Hogarth, Dickens could "quote" or allude to the engravings in order to enrich his own text. This chapter demonstrates Dickens' creative adaptations of Hogarth, adaptations which include, but are not coterminous with, the grotesque.

In a lengthy commentary on "Gin Lane" Dickens observed that the moral implications of Hogarth's well-known engraving were still as apt as they had been:

> It is remarkable of that picture, that while it exhibits drunkenness in its most appalling forms, it forces on the attention of the spectator a most neglected, wretched neighbourhood (the same that is only just now cleared away for the extension of Oxford Street) and an unwholesome, indecent, abject conditon of life.... The church is

> very prominent and handsome, but coldly surveys these things, in progress underneath the shadow of its tower (it was in the year of grace eighteen hundred and forty-eight that a Bishop of London first came out respecting something wrong in poor men's social accommodations), and is passive in the picture. We take all this to have a meaning, and to the best of our knowledge it has not grown obsolete in a century.[13]

That "meaning" might be explained as the presentation of human misery in proximity with impassive institutions. It is the "meaning" Dickens sought to convey in much of his own work.

Like most contemporary writers and artists Dickens was familiar with virtually all of Hogarth's work. He displayed a set of Hogarth's engravings in his home,[14] and the Catalogue of his library listed 48 engravings in his collection.

He and his friends had that kind of easy familiarity with Hogarth's works that enabled them to use the engravings as a ready point of reference. Daniel Maclise once described himself to Dickens as being "in a very bad state of health....my wig off and looking a good deal like that Maniac with his hand to his head in Hogarth's mad scene."[15] Chuckling, Dickens would have known immediately that Mac referred to scene eight from "The Rake's Progress."

Although he could enjoy Hogarthian jokes, Dickens was inclined to take the artist most seriously, for Hogarth had, years earlier, established as a province for art the territory Dickens claimed now for his own. To Mrs. Gore he once described a book he was contemplating which would be in pointed contrast to the fashionable annuals, a book which he conceived in terms of Hogarth:

> What do you think of a book in serious earnest—a true, strong, sledge-hammer book—about the children of the people; as much beaten out of Nature by iron necessity as the children of the nobility are, by luxury and pride? It would be a good thing to have the two extremes—Fairlie and Fielding—Hogarth and Chalon.[16]

Fairlie, a woman who helped edit the fashionable annuals, and Chalon, who was appointed painter in watercolors to the queen, are set in opposition to Fielding and Hogarth, whose work Dickens admired.

As soon as he began publishing, Dickens himself was often compared to Hogarth. "The soul of Hogarth has migrated into the body

William Hogarth, "Gin Lane"

of Mr. Dickens," said Sydney Smith in 1837.[17] R.H. Horne found marked similarity between Hogarth and Dickens, "not substantially nor in particular details, but in moral purpose and finished execution of parts, and of the whole."[18] "What Hogarth was in painting, such very nearly is Mr. Dickens in prose fiction," announced T.H. Lister.[19]

Temperamentally, these two artists separated by several generations shared various characteristics. Frederick Antal has pointed out that these two short men came from humble origins, started as reporters, "and, in a wider sense, both remained reporters of the social scene all their lives."[20]

Aesthetically, their focus and their aim are remarkably similar. Both take urban England and its disadvantaged inhabitants as their primary subject. Both seem intent on bringing those affluent enough to appreciate the arts to acknowledge the presence among them of decidedly unpicturesque elements. Both use the grotesque in order to arouse the awareness of their audience.

Dickens learned some important lessons in using the grotesque effectively from studying Hogarth—and from observing the different ways other graphic artists such as Gillray, Rowlandson, and Cruikshank used it. Hogarth's grotesque was almost always held in check by juxtaposition with a beautiful figure, a practice which had been noted by Coleridge and picked up by Charles Lamb in an essay well known in Dickens' time. Even "in a crowd of humorous deformities" Hogarth included

> a beautiful, usually female, face, which was not meant to act as a contrast, but diffuses through all, and over each of the group, a spirit of reconciliation and human kindness...and thus *prevents the instructive merriment at the whims of nature, or the foibles or humours of our fellowmen, from degenerating into the heart-poison of contempt or hatred.*[21]

Dickens' grotesquerie followed the same tactic of maintaining a balance in order to produce the effect not of mere ridicule, but of instruction.

In the presentation of objects Dickens also learned from Hogarth. All of the ancillary ornaments and decorative pictures in a Hogarth engraving "tell" in a manner that contributes to the work's total meaning. Static or seemingly animated, these objects in Hogarth are given a voice. No object in one of Hogarth's progresses is there merely for decorative effect, just as no object in a Dickens scene is merely ornamental.

Animation enters the Hogarthian, and the Dickensian, scene not just through these speaking details, but by virtue of their seeming to catch the action just at its dramatically critical point. Both of these artists are theatrical, and their introduction of a dramatic technique into essentially static art forms contributes to the sense of movement. This feature of Hogarth's work had been noted by Hazlitt in a much-quoted essay:

> Everything in his pictures has life and motion in it. Not only does the business of the scene never stand still, but every feature and muscle is put into full play; the exact feeling of the moment is brought out, and carried to its utmost height, and then instantly seized and stamped on the canvas for ever. The expression is always taken *en passant,* in a state of progress or change, and, as it were, at the salient point.[22]

The emphasis on action and on catching characters *"en passant"* in a heightened state of emotion, has often been noted as a distinguishing mark of Dickens' art. Here, again, Dickens' contemporaries saw his resemblance to Hogarth.

The dramatic method, the speaking detail, and the use of the grotesque all lead to a controlled exaggeration intended to heighten reality. Harry P. Marten has observed that in contrast to Gillray, "William Hogarth and Charles Dickens began with the familiar world and used exaggeration in order to achieve a final expanded sense of verisimilitude."[23]

This heightening that is a necessary part of their art led both to face the charge of caricature, a charge both took some pains to deny, for it was essential to their purpose that the audience believe in the essential truth they sought to portray.[24] If the audience thought the work a mere burlesque (Fielding's term) of reality, they would feel no involvement, no need to take seriously the situation put before them. No moralist can afford to be thought a mere caricaturist. As Dickens put it in the 1844 Preface to *Martin Chuzzlewit:*

> It is almost needless to add, that the commoner the folly or the crime which an author endeavors to illustrate, the greater is the risk he runs of being charged with exaggeration; for, as no man ever yet re-

> cognized an imitation of himself, no man will admit the correctness of a sketch in which his own character is delineated, however faithfully.[25]

Dickens had already encountered some hostile reaction to *Nicholas Nickleby* (1839), first in charges of exaggeration, then in threats of libel from several Yorkshire schoolmasters convinced Dickens had explicitly drawn them. Similarly, *Oliver Twist* had drawn fire for its topographical description of Jacob's Island, a place one London alderman foolishly dismissed as fictive. For the illustration of Dombey, Dickens had Phiz submit numerous drawings, after studying the features of a number of different models, for the writer was determined no one should accuse him of creating a caricature. Dombey had to be accepted as being essentially real.

John Ruskin, whose estimate of Dickens' talent and his grotesquerie varied with the time of his writing, said in his most quoted remark on Dickens' artistry:

> The essential value and truth of Dickens' writings have been unwisely lost sight of by many thoughtful persons, merely because he presents his truth with some colour of caricature. Unwisely, because Dickens's caricature, though often gross, is never mistaken.... I wish that he could think it right to limit his brilliant exaggeration to works written only for public amusement [and not for *Hard Times*] .... But let us not lose the insight of Dickens's wit and insight, because he chooses to speak in a circle of stage fire.[26]

Ruskin's defense of Dickens' essential truth is much like Fielding's defense of Hogarth in his preface to *Joseph Andrews.* While Fielding emphasized Hogarth's capacity to paint man thinking over man burlesqued (or caricatured), Ruskin defends Dickens' exaggeration as an indispensable part of his truth.

In certain respects Dickens was thought by contemporaries to surpass Hogarth. T.H. Lister said, "Mr. Dickens is exempt from two of Hogarth's least agreeable qualities—his cynicism and his coarseness. There is no misanthropy in his satire, and no coarseness in his descriptions—a merit enhanced by the nature of his subjects."[27]

Victorian delicacy was also reflected in Horne's remark that "in dealing with repulsive characters and actions, Hogarth sometimes does so in a repulsive manner.... Dickens never does this."[28] In winning such praise Dickens succeeded precisely where his painter friends failed;[29] he managed to draw Hogarthian characters in Hogarthian situations and yet gain the reputation of being less coarse and vulgar than his famous predecessor. It was a delicate balancing trick in a prudish era.

Dickens early learned that subtle allusion to Hogarth could enable him to suggest what he never could say. In *Nicholas Nickleby,* for instance, Dickens parodies plate II of "Marriage a la Mode" in which the young married couple, already jaded from their union, sit apart looking visibly bored, with a breakfast tray between them and signs of last night's dissipation scattered about. Dickens describes a highly similar scene, upper-class apartments in a state of disarray after the evening entertainments, inhabited not by young marrieds, but by "Lord Frederick Verisopht and his friend Sir Mulberry Hawk," whose posture and demeanor unmistakably recall Hogarth.

> These distinguished gentlemen were reclining listlessly on a couple of sofas, with a table between them, on which were scattered in rich confusion the materials of an untasted breakfast. Newspapers lay strewn about the room, but these, like the meal, were neglected and unnoticed; not, however, because any flow of conversation prevented the attractions of the journals from being called into request, for not a word was exchanged between the two, nor was any sound uttered, save when one, in tossing about to find an easier resting-place for his aching head, uttered an exclamation of impatience.
>
> Ch. 26

Dickens has placed his characters in exactly the same circumstances as Hogarth's married couple, and though he goes on to describe more extensive remnants of a "debauch"' the parallel still holds. When motion interrupts the still life of the scene, the gesture of Verisopht directly resembles that of the young wife. "Lord Frederick Verisopht was the first to speak. Dropping his slippered foot on the ground, and yawning heavily, he struggled into a sitting posture, and turned his dull languid eyes towards his friend" (Ch. 26). Not only does the parody underscore Verisopht's effeminacy, it also subtly suggests homosexual innuendoes unmentionable in the Victorian period.

Through Hogarthian allusion Dickens gained texture in his work while announcing to his readers that the world of his fiction was the world of one of their most esteemed artists. What Dickens saw and

William Hogarth, "Marriage a la Mode," Plate 2

chose to describe in London is like Hogarth's London—not, generally speaking, the grand thoroughfares and elegant gardens—not a postcard impression—but places of teeming life where what is *said* to be significant is shown in fact to be peripheral. In "The Four Times of Day: Morning," for instance, Hogarth draws a spinster walking to church past a lusty group of citizens who in all probability have not been to bed. She is doing the acceptable thing, but the rigidity of her body suggests better than words can say that she is woodenly observing the proprieties—not learning from them, but observing them only. For she ignores the outstretched hand of the beggar woman right in front of her.

This disparity between what society says one should do (in this case, attend church) and what the people actually do (beg, establish markets, indulge in sensual play) is the wellspring of Dickens' art, just as of Hogarth's. From his earliest writing Dickens' angle of vision was not only similar to but affected by Hogarth. *Sketches by Boz* contains essays which reveal that the life Dickens studied was much like that which interested Hogarth. "The Streets—Morning" describes activities common to the marketplace, and drawn by Hogarth: "men are shouting... boys fighting, basket-women talking, piemen expatiating on the excellence of their pastry." Activity of various sorts simultaneously fills the scene, just as in Hogarth's crowded print. Dickens closes his sketch with an observation which seems to sum up Hogarth's picture: "The streets are thronged with a vast concourse of people, gay and shabby, rich and poor, idle and industrious; and we come to the heat, bustle, and activity of noon."

1. HEIGHTENED REALITY: *OLIVER TWIST*

Dickens' earliest planned narrative, *Oliver Twist* (1838), is markedly Hogarthian, from its preface right into the turbulent London street scenes. This underworld was not one familiar to Dickens' readers, and, to protect himself against the charge of fabrication or exaggeration, he invoked Hogarth. In the 1841 Preface to the third edition Dickens dissociates himself from the popular criminal novel:

> I had read of thieves by scores—seductive fellows (amiable for the most part), faultless in dress, plump in pocket, choice in horseflesh,

bold in bearing, fortunate in gallantry, great at a song, a bottle, pack of cards or dice-box, and fit companions for the bravest. But I had never met (except in HOGARTH) with the miserable reality.

Dickens endeavored to bring the crime-producing conditions of the poor to the attention of the reading public:

> It appeared to me that to draw a knot of such associates in crime as really do exist; to paint them in all their deformity, in all their wretchedness, in all the squalid poverty of their lives; to show them as they really are, for ever skulking uneasily through the dirtiest paths of life, with the great, black, ghastly gallows closing up their prospects, turn them where they may—it appeared to me that to do this would be to attempt a something which was greatly needed and which would be a service to society. And therefore I did it as I best could.

Dickens' underworld characters live with panache, but without real hope. "The great, black, ghastly gallows closing up their prospects" seems to predestine their lives. He had certain precedents in English authors who "brought upon the scene the very scum and refuse of the land," but the greatest, fullest obligation he acknowledges is to Hogarth:

> Hogarth, the moralist, and censor of his age—in whose great works the times in which he lived and the characters of every time will never cease to be reflected—did the like, without the compromise of a hair's breadth, with a power and depth of thought which belonged to few men before him and will probably appertain to fewer still in time to come.

The young Dickens takes hope in recalling that the artist now esteemed a "giant" once endured reproach for exaggerating. Dickens' desire, like Cervantés', is "to dim the false glitter surrounding something which really did exist by showing it in its unattractive and repulsive truth."

Dickens had chosen[30] to write in a highly popular vein known as the Newgate novel. A genre that flourished between 1830 and 1847, the Newgate novel took as one of its principal characters a criminal. According to Keith Hollingsworth,

> What firmly draws the Newgate novels together is that most of them met strong opposition on the ground of morality or taste. Other faults might be alleged against them, but the general objection was that they familiarized their readers with vice and crime, perhaps to a degree socially dangerous.[31]

The writer intent on showing his comfortable readers a world beyond his garden gate had a perilous path to walk. If he "seemed to arouse an unfitting sympathy for the criminal,"[32] he was condemned for having written a Newgate novel. Yet if he did not sympathize to some extent with his criminal character, he could not expect his reader to understand either the mentality or the circumstances that produced such a character. Dickens, wanting his reader to recognize society's complicity in producing the criminal, allied himself with Hogarth in order to signal that his social satire was intended seriously—not just as an entertainment.

Relying heavily on Hogarth in *Oliver Twist* enabled Dickens to surprise his readers with a redemptive reversal. Examining our Hogarth carefully, we find that the first false step sets the stage, ineluctably, for ruin. If the Idle 'Prentice will sleep on the job, he will end up on Tyburn. If the Rake will not show compassion to his mistress, he will end up mad and alone. Once one is in the criminal environment, no hope for redemption seems likely. In Hogarth's progresses—"Industry and Idleness," "The Harlot's Progress," and "The Rake's Progress," the horrors to which the dissipated, criminal life leads are presented with persuasive, Deuteronomic inevitability. By subtitling *Oliver Twist* "A Parish Boy's Progress" Dickens seems to signal a similar sort of moral tale.

The Hogarthian allusions in the preface and the Hogarthian form of the subtitle prepare us for a story line that works its determined way toward demonstrating the irrevocable link between poverty, crime, and the gallows. The world on which *Oliver Twist* opens is like the world of the last two plates of "The Harlot's Progress:" funereal, lugubrious, impoverished, and full of hypocrisy. In those lowly circumstances certain characters are seeking ways of gaining an advantage over others, or are solacing themselves with the means commonly available to the poor in Dickens' time as in Hogarth's: gin.[33] The dying mother and orphaned son receive little attention from the other characters either in Hogarth or in Dickens. What really absorbs their interest is pillaging for some token of value, arguing the value of one potion over another, or contemplating alcohol. Dickens exactly captures that displacement of concern from the human to the material. His ancillary characters, like Hogarth's, are satirized through the discrepancy between their sanctimonious dress and expression on the one hand, and their selfish or sensuous behavior on the other.

When Oliver's mother dies, the attendant doctor regards her as but another unwed mother and her orphaned son as but another unwanted burden on the parish. The attendant nurse, Mrs. Thingummy, evidences more concern for the alcohol in her "green glass bottle" than for the troublesome infant. Both of these characters have their antecedents in "The Harlot's Progress;" the doctor resembles the posturing quack in Plate V who evinces not the slightest concern for the dying Moll; while Mrs. Thingummy resembles Hogarth's bawd in the lower right-hand corner of Plate VI who keeps the brandy bottle within sight while feigning grief at the death of Moll.

Bumble the Beadle and Sowerberry the undertaker are presented as a pair of contrasts that recall the quack doctors attending "The Dying Harlot." Bumble is "a fat man, and a choleric one" (Ch. 2) who has gold-laced cuffs and carries a cane, the very details characterizing Hogarth's rotund gentleman. Sowerberry "was a tall, gaunt, large-jointed man." Like the thin doctor holding a small jar in Hogarth, Sowerberry carries a box of snuff, a box Dickens elaborates into "an ingenious little model of a patent coffin" (Ch. 4).

Ironic commentary on the scene often occurs in Hogarth's details: the coat of arms in Plate VI of "The Harlot's Progress," for instance; Bumble's buttons are used with similar effect. Sowerberry notices and admires them, leading Bumble to explain, "The die is the same as the parochial seal—the Good Samaritan healing the sick and bruised man" (Ch. 4). This sanctimonious and ludicrously inaccurate identification serves as one of the primary means of satirizing Bumble. No one but a grotesque would be known chiefly through his buttons.

With the introduction of Mr. Brownlow the novel evokes the double Hogarthian progress that traces both a successful rise and a dismal decline: "Industry and Idleness." Oliver's history to this point, as observed by the parish authorities, seems to lead toward the destiny of Thomas Idle: transportation by sea, and later, death by hanging.

William Hogarth, "A Harlot's Progress," Plate 5

William Hogarth, "A Harlot's Progress," Plate 6

But suddenly, miraculously, Oliver is placed in a positive environment, though not securely. The alternation among Brownlow's town-house, Fagin's den, and Rose Maylie's cottage suggests the contrasting environments of Francis Goodchild and Thomas Idle.[34] There is, of course, a good deal of the fortuitous in Oliver's history, whereas Hogarth was attempting to show, albeit ironically,[35] the penalties and rewards of ease or effort. Dickens' alternate environments carry a considerable element of terror, for the passage from comfort to despair is so abrupt, so unpredictable, and hence so grotesque.

Dickens, altering the pattern of Hogarthian reference that he had purposely established, holds out the possibility of moral improvement. With faith in the power of love to effect salutary change, Dickens leads innocent Oliver to a better life. In *Oliver Twist* the redemption works miraculously, through stock devices such as mistaken identities that are resolved through the mysterious resemblance of a portrait, and the curious circulation of a ring. This contrived resolution plays to every child's unspoken hope that he or she was actually born into more auspicious circumstances than those in which he or she is forced to live. It is the pattern traced by many fairy tales, but the Hogarthian structures make it considerably more than that.

Dickens had learned well the lesson taught by Hogarth and observed by Coleridge and Lamb that the inclusion of beauty within scenes of misery has a beneficent effect. Through Nancy, the slatternly creature whose compassion for Oliver exacts her life, Dickens introduces a sense for higher principles even among ruffians. He was criticized extensively for what was thought his sentimentalizing, but he defended himself in his customary manner by insisting on the truth of his presentation:

> It is useless to discuss whether the conduct and character of the girl seems natural or unnatural, probable or improbable, right or wrong. It is true.... It is emphatically God's truth, for it is the Truth He leaves in such depraved and miserable breasts, the hope yet lingering behind, the last fair drop of water at the bottom of the dried-up weed-choked well. It involves the best and worst shades of our common nature, much of its ugliest hues and something of its most beautiful; it is a contradiction, an anomaly, an apparent impossibility, but it is a truth. I am glad to have had it doubted, for in that circumstance I find a sufficient assurance that it needed to be told.[36]

Dickens' belief in the possibility of goodness even among the lowest is at the root of his reformist impulse. But it was also for him, as for Hogarth, an artistic necessity to present beauty amid squalor. He goes so far as to suggest that poor, slatternly Nancy might have adapted to a virtuous pattern. The possibility being so remote, however, Dickens has to kill her off.

In *Oliver Twist* Dickens, like Hogarth, shows the pernicious effects of an unsalutary environment,[37] but he also shows that these unhappy effects are at least partially reversible. If the human character can be undermined, Dickens shows us that it can also be restored. He does not diminish the negative power of poverty to warp character, but he does hold out the possibility—however remote—that the hapless victim may be capable of reform. Dickens' vision is essentially New Testament in its insistence that latent goodness lurks in the breasts of most individuals.

This redemptive pattern is enacted throughout the fiction, most baldly in *A Christmas Carol.* Maintaining this hope against such insuperable odds is, indeed, one of Dickens' most endearing traits, for it enables us to believe not only in the redemptive qualities in our world, but in ourselves. While life lasts, there remains hope of change—if we are to accept Dickens—and the New Testament.

2. THE HIDDEN REALITY: *DOMBEY AND SON*

The world of Mr. Dombey is one of projected propriety. He wants, and his social standing demands, the Victorian ideal: placidly domestic wife and obedient, line-preserving son. Both relations will substantiate his social position and insure a kind of material immortality; the institutions he has built and served are thus to survive in his heir. A daughter, being quite worthless in this generation-spanning scheme, can be ignored. And is.

What Dombey desires and what he receives are obviously divergent from the outset. His placid wife dies; his son is sickly; and his useless daughter is an irritant. Yet Dombey doggedly adheres to the fictive image of family life and goes to considerable lengths to achieve this ideal.

Browne's first two plates show the initial disparity with which the novel begins. We first see the Toodles family, numerous round-cheeked children grouped comfortingly near their parents. The next plate, "The Dombey Family," shows Mrs. Toodles, now "Richards," holding the son and heir to one side while Mr. Dombey sits stiffly distanced in the center of the room and Florence assumes a humble stance out of her father's sight, yet disturbingly in his presence nonetheless. Clearly this is a family in name only.

The opening scene of the novel establishes the disparity between Dombey's image of the world and the actualities of the situation. With masterful irony Dickens has Dombey himself, in his first utterance, express the sense of discrepancy:

> "The House will once again, Mrs. Dombey," said Mr. Dombey, "be not only in name but in fact Dombey and Son;" and he added, in a tone of luxurious satisfaction, with his eyes half-closed as if he were reading the name in a device of flowers, and inhaling their fragrance at the same time; "Dombey and Son!"

The picturesque embellishments Dombey imagines surrounding the fictive name of Dombey and Son prevent his recognizing the fact of his daughter. Name and fact do not coincide in this book. While Walter Gay recognized early that the firm's title really should be "Dombey—and Son—and Daughter!" (Ch. 4), Dombey himself needs be brought so low as to contemplate suicide before he fully realizes the distinction between name and fact.

That slow, agonizing process of education is necessary not just for Dombey, but for the reader as well. Great social significance attaches to the "fact" first expressed by Miss Tox in heartbroken tone "that Dombey and Son should be a Daughter after all!" (Ch. 16). Towards the end of the book Miss Tox repeats her observation, but without lament (Ch. 59).

A funny little minor character dares to name what is fact. Her doing so carries meaning considerably beyond the necessities of the plot. The name Dombey and Daughter inverts a pattern of male dominance, male expectations, and male glory assumed by western man since he began to write. By dramatizing the gradual merger of the factual presence of intelligent, compassionate women with the naming of them as partners in the society, Dickens demonstrates remarkable sensitivity to the plight of the second sex and shows a certain prescience regarding the winds of change then gathering storm.

In this novel Dickens reveals the human cost involved in social organization that stresses proper appearance to the exclusion of emotional needs. At the very height of industrialism and belief in progress, Dickens suggests that their virtues are illusory. The old verities of compassion and sympathetic understanding cannot be merely swept away by the press of business and the expectation of profits. Or, if human emotion is disregarded, the penalty exacted is nothing less than a human life.

Dombey and Son discovers a number of disparities between assumption and fact in the newly industrializing society, a society which promotes an image of itself out of keeping with reality. To expose that falsity Dickens alludes to Hogarth, to several interwoven narrative series, as well as to individual works.

The first clear instance in *Dombey and Son* where Dickens draws a Hogarthian picture is in the ceremony marking Paul's christening. The ceremonies marking our rites of passage are expected to follow certain patterns, yet it is in the divergence from the expected that much can be told about character. Hogarth was a master at catching characters in the precise moment of behaving inappropriately to the demands of the occasion, and Dickens adapts this technique of showing visually the inadequacy of character.

Early in the novel Mr. Dombey's primary inadequacy is his lack of heart, and the inhuman attitude he assumes is visibly apparent—especially at the christening where his vaunted self-sufficiency is at its height. To his sister he declares,

> "Paul and myself will be able, when the time comes, to hold our own—the House, in other words, will be able to hold its own, and maintain its own, and hand down its own of itself, and without any such common-place aids. The kind of foreign help which people usually seek for their children, I can afford to despise; being above it, I hope."
>
> Ch. 5

Dombey's vanity and his excessive pride form a barrier between him and other human beings, a barrier he enforces by making himself so austere, so cold, so formidable as to be comparable rather with inhuman elements:

William Hogarth, "The Christening"

> Mr. Dombey represented in himself the wind, the shade, and the autumn of the christening. He stood in his library to receive the company, as hard and cold as the weather; and when he looked out through the glass room, at the trees in the little garden, their brown and yellow leaves came fluttering down, as if he blighted them.... The stiff and stark fire-irons appeared to claim a nearer relationship than anything else there to Mr. Dombey.

Dombey has made himself a grotesque, a being comparable not to living creatures, but to things and forces of inhuman nature.

The distance Dombey places between himself and the other members of the christening party recalls the distance between the foppish father and the other participants in Hogarth's "Christening," particularly as the other characters dispose themselves in a manner clearly evocative of the picture. Young Paul, in the company of the Chicks, Miss Tox, and Susan, bursts into tears, and Florence is urged by her aunt to entertain him.

> The atmosphere became or might have become colder and colder, when Mr. Dombey stood frigidly watching his little daughter, who, clapping her hands, and standing on tip-toe before the throne of his son and heir, lured him to bend down from his high estate, and look at her.

Unlike her Hogarthian prototype Florence does not upset the baptismal water, but her active engagement in the scene does emphasize her father's distance from it, just as the foolish father in Hogarth remains disengaged. Thus does frigid pride achieve the same end as foppish vanity.

When the Dombey party goes to church, they enter another markedly Hogarthian scene, one that recalls the Wedding of the Rake:

> The very wedding looked dismal as they passed in front of the altar. The bride was too old and the bridegroom too young, and a superannuated beau with one eye and an eyeglass stuck in its blank companion, was giving away the lady, while the friends were shivering.

Both of these Hogarthian scenes are marked by considerable disparity. The ceremony taking place has nothing humanly sacramental

William Hogarth, "The Rake's Progress," Plate 5

about it. What Dickens seizes on in both pictures is the inhuman aloofness of Dombey, the self-absorbed pride that causes him to freeze out everyone else:

> It might have been well for Mr. Dombey, if he had thought of his own dignity a little less; and had thought of the great origin and purpose of the ceremony in which he took so formal and so stiff a part, a little more. His arrogance contrasted strangely with its history.

When they return for a celebratory feast, Dombey's cold arrogance is more strongly felt. So warped has he become that he casts a deathly, icy pall over everyone. "The party seemed to get colder and colder, and to be gradually resolving itself into a congealed and solid state, like the collation round which it was assembled." People are reduced to frozen objects in the glow of Dombey's presence.[38]

Dombey inadvertently creates a sense of grotesquerie around him, even while attempting to observe custom decorously. Withholding love from those nearest him, Dombey subverts the natural warmth of human intimacy into the unnatural chill of a frozen dinner. This transformation of the animate into the inanimate is a mark of the grotesque. Yet living with this has not prepared Florence for another sort of grotesquerie she encounters outside what she calls her home.

"Good Old Mrs. Brown" carries a name which masks her reality, for she is neither kind nor married. Far from offering Florence the motherly solicitude that seems implicit in her name, Mrs. Brown transforms her from elegantly appareled child of the apparent rich to beggarly child of utter neglect, metamorphosing her physically to match the emotional reality. The scene bears striking resemblance to Hogarth's "New Metamorphosis" wherein we see a soot-darkened room, piles of rags, a witch, a frightened young girl, and a slightly older lad, who might serve to rescue her. In Dickens' narrative Florence flees to Walter, who recognizes her despite her metamorphosis, and restores her to the home which, if unloving, is at least more secure than the hovel to which she was abducted.

Mr. Dombey's distorted values and perceptions are presented to us visually in several scenes evocative of Hogarthian pictures. That visually realized sense of disparity is developed throughout a plot structure that is in effect a merging of several Hogarthian progresses: "Marriage a la Mode,"[39] reflected in the disastrous encounter between

William Hogarth, "The New Metamorphosis"

Dombey and Edith; "The Rake's Progress," reflected in the Carker and Alice plot; and "Industry and Idleness," reflected in the contrast between Rob the Grinder and Walter Gay, as well as between the two Carker brothers. "The Harlot's Progress" informs the briefly narrated events of Alice Brown's life. Not only do these series help to organize the plot into a cohesive entity, but their allusive presence lends texture and interest to the novel, extending its suggestiveness from the immediate focus of the plot to the society at large.

Dickens uses these Hogarthian patterns very like a modern mythology, a set of shared stories that establish a cluster of expectations which he can adapt, alter, or invert. "Marriage a la Mode" lends both structure and detail to the story of Dombey's second marriage. Like the arranged marriage in Hogarth (and society at large) it is considered "a good match on both sides; for she had beauty, blood, and talent, and Dombey had fortune" (Ch. 26). Yet, shortly after Major Bagstock makes this observation, the unsuitability of the match is told visually through a scene evocative of the first plate of "Marriage a la Mode." Standing in a gallery at Warwick Castle, Edith and Dombey are such discordant personalities

> that fancy might have imagined the pictures on the walls around them, startled by the unnatural conjunction, and observant of it in their several expressions. Grim knights and warriors looked scowling on them. A churchman, with his hand upraised, denounced the mockery of such a couple coming to God's altar. Quiet waters in landscapes, with the sun reflected in their depths, asked, if better means of escape were not at hand, was there no drowning left? Ruins cried, "Look here, and see what We are, wedded to uncongenial Time!" Animals, opposed by nature, worried one another, as a moral to them. Loves and Cupids took to flight afraid, and Martyrdom had no such torment in its painted history of suffering.
>
> Ch. 27

Like their Hogarthian counterparts, the characters are oblivious of the commentary made by the seemingly inanimate, yet speaking, pictures. In order to achieve a certain social standing, both Edith and Dombey ignore the clear warnings of incompatibility, thinking to live a life of quiet respectability, yet unaware they are forming themselves into grotesques by the suppression of instinct and desire.

William Hogarth, "Marriage a la Mode," Plate 1

Respecting the Victorian proprieties, Dickens dissolves the marriage without Hogarthian licentiousness, but he does have Edith run off to the Continent with Carker. Before she flees, Edith parts from her beloved stepdaughter, to whom she is from that time virtually dead, paralleling "The Death of the Countess" in which mother and daughter part. Dombey does not die in a duel in the Bagnio, but he is on the verge of stabbing himself when Florence discovers him.

But while Hogarth's countess appears so shallow a personality as to preclude any genuine sympathy, Dickens' Edith has a fiery spirit and considerable awareness of her situation. On the eve of her marriage she lashes out at her mother for rearing her to such ignominy, to a life in which emotion and deed are forever separated:

> "Look at me," she said, "who have never known what it is to have an honest heart, and love. Look at me, taught to scheme and plot when children play; and married in my youth—an old age of design—to one for whom I had no feeling but indiffence.... There is no slave in a market: there is no horse in a fair: so shown and offered and examined and paraded, Mother, as I have been, for ten shameful years."
> Ch. 27

The appearances to which she has been reared prevail but a short time; then twisted passion bursts forth and brings down the whole edifice. On the night before Edith abandons him, Dombey tells her, "There are appearances in these things which must be maintained before the world" (Ch. 47). The next morning, apprised of her departure, he bursts into her disarrayed room heaped with all her ornaments and gowns, and he turns utterly savage.

The stages of the Dombey marriage and its dissolution are clearly marked, just as in Hogarth, by shifts in rooms—the interior design and the accessory ornaments telling a good deal about the emotional temper of the characters at a particular point. When we next see Edith, she is in France, in an environment marked by a kind of transient tawdriness:

> An air of splendour, sufficiently faded to be melancholy, and sufficiently dazzling to clog and embarrass the details of life with a show of state, reigned in these rooms. The walls and ceilings were gilded and painted; the floors were waxed and polished; crimson drapery hung in festoons from window, door, and mirror; and candelabra,

> gnarled and intertwisted like the branches of trees, or horns of animals, stuck out from the panels of the wall. But in the day-time, when the lattice-blinds (now closely shut) were opened, and the light let in, traces were discernible among this finery, of wear and tear and dust, of sun and damp and smoke, and lengthened intervals of want of use and habitation, when such shows and toys of life seem sensitive like life, and waste as men shut up in prison do.
>
> Ch. 54

The crimson drapery and branching candelabra suggest an adulterous inclination, though Edith commits adultery in appearance only, while the contrasting dreariness of the rooms upon the admission of light suggests the empty, wasted quality of her remaining years.

Back in the Dombey mansion all is changed as well. The grandly refurbished house is dismantled save for one room in which the master lives out his fallen pride. "He wandered through the rooms: lately so luxurious; now so bare and dismal and so changed, apparently, even in their shape and size" (Ch. 59).

Before we consider the alterations Dickens made on the ending of "Marriage a la Mode,"[40] we need to look at the other Hogarthian narratives woven together with the Dombey plot. The other major progress standing behind *Dombey and Son* is "Industry and Idleness," Hogarth's very middleclass presentation of the virtues and rewards associated with hard work, and the vice and punishment associated with laziness. A strongly deterministic cast colors this, as the other Hogarth progresses. Once one is on the road to ruin, the path is unswervingly downwards. When Rob the Grinder says, "I know I've been agoing wrong, Sir, ever since I took to bird-catching and walking-matching" (Ch. 22), it seems we are witnessing an adaptation of the Idle 'Prentice, especially since he takes up with Carker, and since his family laments that "He has fell into bad company" (Ch. 20). When he visits his family, he is labelled "the prodigal son," and they, in turn, think that the man accompanying him is Jack Ketch, the hangman. But Dickens does not let Rob go the way of Thomas Idle. Instead of being transported and later hanged at Tyburn, Rob is redeemed in time by luck and his loving family.

If Rob seems to be cast as the Idle 'Prentice, Walter Gay seems to play the Industrious 'Prentice. He, like Francis Goodchild, is early identified with Dick Whittington who, by dint of hard work and

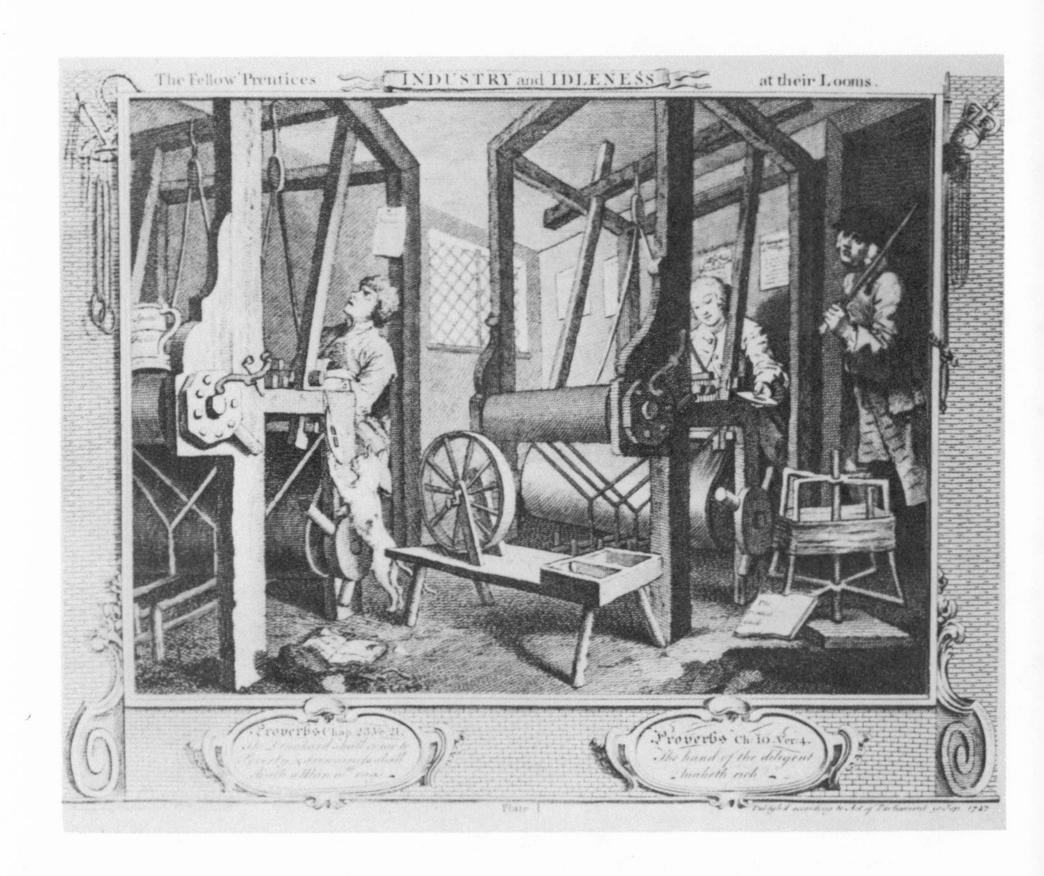

William Hogarth, "Industry and Idleness," Plate I

virtuous conduct, grew up to marry his master's daughter and become Lord Mayor of London. He is contrasted not only with a boy his own age, but with a man a generation older who recognizes the latency for good or ill in the young boy. To his successful brother John Carker says,

> "I have had...my whole heart awakened by my observation of that boy, Walter Gay. I saw in him when he first came here, almost my other self.... Not as I am, but as I was when I first came here too; as sanguine, giddy, youthful, inexperienced; flushed with the same restless and adventurous fancies; and full of the same qualities, fraught with the same capacity of leading on to good or evil."
>
> Ch. 13

John Carker's fortunes are a subdued version of Thomas Idle's in contrast to those of his managerial brother, who is anything but a Goodchild. Carker the Manager has achieved his position by the cunning wiles of a cat to which he is so often compared. Those feline characteristics of slinking, grinning a tooth-filled yet emotionless grin, and even showing claws are marks of the grotesque. Bestial in his personal behavior, savage in his selfishness, Carker brings on his own tragedy by a series of treacherous acts carrying increasingly evil effects. Although he is both more malevolent and more intelligent than Thomas Rakewell, Carker's actions bear a glancing resemblance to Hogarth's Rake, and his name may be anagrammatical.

Long before the story opens, Carker has apparently seduced Alice Marwood (Brown), and then abandoned her, leaving her to a life of petty crimes for which she eventually pays by deportation. With the encouragement of her mother, for which Alice is bitterly reproachful, Alice has sunk into levels of degradation suggestive of "The Harlot's Progress." Thus her response to the sight of Carker elicits something quite different from the sweet loyalty of Hogarth's Sarah Young in "The Rake's Progress."

In Chapter 46 Carker rides his white-legged horse through the streets, his carriage suggestive of the high social state he has reached—though he is soon to fall. Mrs. Brown and Alice watch him pass, the daughter with a hatred screwed toward vengeance, the mother, avaricious still, wishing her daughter would solicit money from him.

William Hogarth, "The Rake's Progress," Plate I

> "See where he goes!" muttered the old woman, watching her daughter with her red eyes; "so easy and so trim, a-horseback, while we are in the mud—"
>
> "And of it," said her daughter impatiently. "We are mud, underneath his horse's feet. What should we be?"

And so the scene is set for the downfall of Carker with the assistance of small Rob the Grinder, Carker's servant.

Hogarth's Rake early appears to be climbing in society and enjoying its perquisites. So, too, Carker, though the seeds of disaster are visible from the outset. Hogarth's Rake loses his wits and dies in Bedlam. Dickens' Carker is on the verge of madness, pursued by felt, but unseen, ghosts when he is struck by a train.[41] Carker's ruin follows a typical Hogarthian pattern of reaping the whirlwind one has sown. Other characters, however, are redeemed by at least some decent action or forgivable motivation.

Alice Marwood, like Hogarth's young harlot, pays for her ruinous life with an early death, yet not without generating some sympathy for her plight. Her poverty, and the unseemly avarice of her mother, have led to her prostitution, but a remarkable scene in Chapter 34 shows us that the same pattern is repeated in the upper classes. At the end of this chapter entitled "Another Mother and Daughter" (a chapter following "Contrasts" and preceding "The Happy Pair," as if to underscore the parallelism of the converging plots), Dickens pointedly explains the connection:

> Were this miserable mother, and this miserable daughter, only the reduction to their lowest grade, of certain social vices sometimes prevailing higher up? In this round world of many circles within circles, do we make a weary journey from the high grade to the low, to find at last that they lie close together, that the two extremes touch, and that our journey's end is but our starting-place? Allowing for great difference of stuff and texture, was the pattern of this woof repeated among gentle blood at all?
>
> Say Edith Dombey! And Cleopatra, best of mothers, let us have your testimony!

The society offered women so few ways of leading a respectable life that they were forced into situations where they must, in effect, if not literally, sell themselves to a man. This emphasis, repeatedly drawn in the patterns of the novel, differs markedly from Hogarth. We begin to see that Dickens is using those Hogarthian patterns not just to organize a complex plot, not just for a mythological overlay of recognizable situations, but to invert them. Not only does Dickens stress a redemptive element quite at odds with the Deuteronomic morality of Hogarth, but he focuses on the feminine protagonists rather than the masculine. These female figures are not mere passive participants in the drama, not simply quiet victims of man's brutish behavior; they are articulate, feeling creatures seeking some means of control over their own lives.

Edith has few options, but she can flee from a loveless marriage, and she can resist becoming the adulterous pawn of yet another man. Through the power of love, Florence manages to connect herself with a worthy man, even though he is beneath her social class; and, again through the power of her love, she redeems her father.

The men in charge of society, as represented by Dombey and Carker, are not about to alter social custom in any way that curtails masculine prerogatives—that is, until they suffer a dramatic change of heart. Dombey must be brought to the edge of suicide and madness, the ultimate of grotesquerie, before his adamantine heart softens to the ministrations of a daughter. He is emblematic of his time. Nothing less than a painful change of heart will reform a social structure elevating men into a position of financial mastery over women and children. That image of society is a grotesque monstrosity, as Dickens shows us with his Hogarthian patterns.[42]

While these patterns rest behind *Dombey and Son,* linking together disparate narrative strains and providing richness of texture, the most significant feature of their presence is the way in which Dickens varies them. Unexpected outcomes to Hogarthian patterns appeared in *Oliver Twist,* but there the goodness of Oliver seemed a New Testament importation verging on the miraculous. Dickens' method in *Dombey and Son* is more realistic, and he varies the Hogarthian pattern not only to show the complexities of mid-century life, but also to suggest the necessary complementarity of men and women. One of the unhappy consequences of modern life is the single-minded focus on institutional success that obliterates personal life and freezes the emotions. (It is a problem Dickens considers again in *Great Expectations.*) Achieving a proper balance between what the nineteenth-century thought of as feminine feeling and masculine ambition is no small task and, if we look at Carker and Dombey, we are brought to the conclusion that such a balance may be virtually impossible.

Can an ambitious person achieve professional success and maintain warm personal relationships at the same time? Or does family life necessarily decline as professional ambition climbs? Dickens' happiest people in *Dombey and Son* are the Toodles, the Sol Gills—those living at a lower or superceded level of the economy.

The questions Dickens raises here are deeply disturbing, and not readily answered. Dombey becomes a better man by admitting his emotional being—but it takes a complete professional collapse to bring about his transformation of character. Edith, on the other hand, might have had a chance to develop as a human being had she had more than the traditional female opportunities available to her.

Establishing a society in which Dombey and Daughter might serve together as equal partners, in which their talents, their drive, and their compassion are equally tapped, was beyond Dickens' imagining (and, so far, beyond our realization)—though he had the prescience to anticipate some of the ancillary problems. Dickens, with his eighteenth-century Hogarthian patterns, raised questions for his own time that have continuing reverberations in our own.

Chapter Three
The Dance of Death

DICKENS USED the Dance of Death, particularly Holbein's version of it, much as he used Hogarth: to jar his readers into recognizing the moral implications of certain patterns of behavior. The Dance of Death is the ultimate of grotesque modes, for it directly confronts the living with their deepest fear: Death entering unexpectedly makes a mockery of the pretenses by which we live. Sham, deception, surface all crumble before the approach of this most feared, most grotesque, yet most real interruption. There is no image more grotesque, more out of keeping with one's expectations of what a rich, full life should bring than the image of Death. And in a Christian age, as Dickens' still was, that image carried not just the sense of life's inevitable, though unthinkable, end, but of a summons to answer for one's deeds before one's Creator.

Flashing images of the Dance of Death appear from *The Pickwick Papers* through *The Mystery of Edwin Drood,* but in *Dombey and Son* such imagery is central to the meaning of the book. It serves to define the moral hollowness of several characters, sometimes by traditional means, sometimes by highly inventive excursions from the tradition. Mrs. Skewton's elaborate pretension of preserved youth is not merely a sign of female vanity, but, through the association of images from the Dance of Death, an indicator of the most profound lack of self-knowledge and a consequent inversion of values.

One of the ways in which our age differs most markedly from Dickens' must be in our attitudes toward death. Paradoxically we seem to tolerate nearly perpetual warfare, the expectation of atomic annihilation, and movies of increasingly ingenious means of destructtion—yet death as an actual occurrence affecting our personal lives has virtually no reality for us. We have to be taught—by a whole new emerging industry of writers, workshops, and specially trained nurses—to deal with death, or else turn the whole unpleasant business over to an antiseptic institution.

In Dickens' age death was still a religious event, and as such it had a meaning and a relation that seem to have been obliterated in our time. Dickens' contemporaries were still capable of being moved by the medieval Dance of Death, not just because of their familiarity with its artistic depictions, but because their religious beliefs still accepted many of the same premises. In Dickens' still Christian era Death serves a summons to appear before the Creator and to answer for one's activities. Death as a conductor between the earthly and the eternal is a far more terrifying figure than Death as a signalman announcing journey's end.

The origins of the Dance of Death are obscure, though it seems likely that an actual dance, as part of a drama, was involved.[1] Scholars agree that the earliest pictorial version was a 1424 mural at the cemetery of the Church of the Holy Innocents in Paris. Various interpretations of the theme in murals and books appeared during the fifteenth century, but it was Hans Holbein the Younger (1497–1543) who interpreted the Dance of Death so forcefully that new editions of his book are still being printed.

Holbein's *Les Simulachres et Historiees Faces de la Mort* was completed in 1526 and first published in Lyons in 1538. The book was immensely popular in England, where Holbein spent the last years of his life, with many reprints in the late eighteenth and early nineteenth centuries. Accompanying each of the engravings were Bible verses and bits of poetry (the author of which remains obscure), the idea being to persuade readers by word and picture to live according to holy law.

Dickens was first exposed to Holbein's book when his uncle lent him a copy.[2] A subsequent library slip from the British Museum indicates Dickens checked out Holbein's Dance of Death in 1832 or 1833.[3] The edition he saw at the British Museum, and the one he bought for his own library in 1841, was engraved by W. Hollar and published by Francis Douce. It was a highly popular edition in Dickens' time.[4]

Holbein made each of his original 41 scenes (another 17, especially the latter putti are of disputed origin)[5] highly dramatic, fully detailed, and filled with emotional intensity that seems to move. As Aldred Scott Warthin puts it,

> These are pictures of life rather than of death. He shows us no representation of the actual death scene; his demonic forms of death serve only to illuminate and to heighten the energy of life. At the first glance his pictures may seem to be simple depictions of death scenes; but a moment's contemplation convinces us that their chief interest lies in their dramatic expression of life, and not in the horror or the inevitableness of death.[6]

Few of Death's victims, from high to low, meet his sudden arrival willingly, yet Death the Leveller, Death the Powerful, dances each away. There is often macabre humor in Death's posture, his pleasure in his grisly task contrasting sharply with the victim's horror at such ultimate rudeness. This macabre humor, held in check by Holbein's serious purpose, runs away in several nineteenth-century versions.

Thomas Bewick drew a free interpretation of Holbein's engravings in 1789 with English verses. But the first real English versions of the Dance of Death did not appear until the next century, and then there were two, both comic, both using contemporary dress and scenes. Warthin points out that "there is a tendency to caricaturize the subjects of the Dance of Death; and this tendency asserted itself predominantly in the first thirty years of the nineteenth century, and especially in England."[7] Richard Dagley's "Death's Doing" (1826) put Death in a modern setting, but enjoyed less popularity than the earlier version by Thomas Rowlandson and William Combe. "The English Dance of Death" came out in a series from 1814-1816 by the collaborators of the picturesque satire "The Tour of Dr. Syntax in Search of the Picturesque" (1809). In the updated version the English caricaturist treated Death as an object of ridicule, a foolish figure who interrupts contemporary life, albeit rudely. Moral satire such as that which informs Holbein's work is largely lacking in Rowlandson's. Rather than reminding readers to live with dignity and compassion, Death in Rowlandson's prints merely serves to link disparate scenes of English life.

The terrible juxtaposition of Death and Life is more poignantly and more seriously realized in Holbein than in Rowlandson. Death signals a solemn calling to account in Holbein, but in Rowlandson Death reduces everything to the level of banality. There is the mood of the music hall rather than the hushed solemnity of the cathedral. Holbein's backgrounds, with their medieval architecture and old-fashioned dress, elicit the world of Gothic cathedrals, but more than the peripheral detail encourages a deeply serious interpretation. The disposition of the figures themselves has a certain dignity. Not so in Rowlandson, where we witness the sporting life of the gentry, and the lusty gratification of the senses.

The existence of a contemporary interpretation of the Dance of Death may have suggested fictional possibilities to Dickens, but his own imagery more often reflects the vision of Holbein than of Rowlandson. Deeply committed to a moral view of art, and intent on revealing the hidden consequences of immoral behavior, Dickens adapted the work of Holbein which gave clear visual expression to the same idea.

Early in his writing career Dickens began to explore the narrative, visual, and moral possibilities in the Dance of Death. The 1847 Preface to *The Pickwick Papers* alludes to a plate from Holbein:

> The universal diffusion of common means of decency and health is as much the right of the poorest of the poor, as it is indispensable to the safety of the rich, and of the State; that a few petty boards and bodies—less than drops in the great ocean of humanity, which roars around them—are not for ever to let loose Fever and Consumption on God's creatures at their will, or always to keep their jobbing little fiddles going, for a Dance of Death.

Dickens treats the figure of fiddling Death in Holbein's "Expulsion" as the personification of the rich, the controlling powers of society who make life a Death Dance for the poor.

The Preface alludes to only a part of *The Pickwick Papers*—not to the slapstick adventures of Pickwick and company, but to the inserted dark tales which speak of social injustice.[8] One of these tales clearly in the Dance of Death tradition is "The Stroller's Tale," whose central character closely resembles Rowlandson's "Pantomime" clown.

> He was dressed for the pantomime, in all the absurdity of a clown's costume. The spectral figures in the Dance of Death, the most frightful shapes that the ablest painter ever portrayed on canvas, never presented an appearance half so ghastly. His bloated body and shrunken legs—their deformity enhanced a hundred fold by the fantastic dress—the glassy eyes, contrasting fearfully with the thick white paint with which the face was besmeared; the grotesquely ornamented head, trembling with paralysis, and the long, skinny hands, rubbed with white chalk—all gave him a hideous and unnatural appearance, of which no description could convey an adequate idea.
>
> Ch. III

Rowlandson's pantomime clown is dressed in white, and Dickens' clown wears white makeup; Rowlandson's figure, like Dickens', has distorted features, and somewhat "glassy eyes" starting out of his head in fear and revulsion as Death approaches. The clown and several cronies appear in the picture to have trembling old heads, while the hands of one are "long and skinny." Various of the visual features drawn by Rowlandson and described by Dickens coincide, but the intention behind the two appears quite different. Whereas no discernible moral statement arises out of Rowlandson's picture, the description and setting of Dickens' clown are intended as a moral rebuke to society. The clown lives by entertaining others, by providing pleasure, regardless of his own feelings; but the people he entertains are oblivious of his great personal need, unconcerned about the conditions under which he lives—or dies—because unaware of them.

Dickens makes his Rowlandsonian clown carry a moral meaning well beyond anything the caricaturist ever intended. Similarly, Dickens' description of Anthony Chuzzlewit bears marked resemblance to a figure from *The English Dance of Death*, but again carries significantly richer moral meaning:

> Old Anthony, dressed in his usual clothes, was in the room—beside the table. He leaned upon the shoulder of his solitary friend; and on

Hans Holbein, "The Expulsion from Paradise"

Thomas Rowlandson, "The Pantomime"

> his livid face, and on his horny hands, and in his glassy eyes, and traced by an eternal finger in the very drops of sweat upon his brow, was one word—Death.
>
> *Martin Chuzzlewit,* Ch. 18

The very characteristics made prominent in Rowlandson's drawing of "The Miser" distinguish Dickens' Anthony: "horny hands," "glassy eye," and blue-gray, i.e., "livid face." No one manages any genuine grief at Anthony's demise. Mourners hired by Mr. Mould make up the public cortege, and the professional wake-sitter, Mrs. Gamp, performs the private duties which should have come from family piety.

The unlamented passing of the Rowlandsonian Anthony is echoed in the end Dickens accords other misers. Nicholas Nickleby's Uncle Ralph unfeelingly withholds the financial assistance he could so easily give, and earns the reward of finding his life unbearable. Preoccupied by the memory of having once sat on a jury for a suicide victim, Ralph wanders by a burial ground for the poor and witnesses a spontaneous Dance of Death:

> While he was thus engaged, there came towards him, with noise of shouts and singing, some fellows full of drink, followed by others who were remonstrating with them and urging them to go home in quiet. They were in high good-humour; and one of them, a little, weazen, hump-backed man, began to dance. He was a grotesque fantastic figure, and the few bystanders laughed. Ralph himself was moved to mirth, and echoed the laugh of one who stood near and who looked round in his face. When they had passed on, and he was left alone again, he resumed his speculation with a new kind of interest; for he recollected that the last person who had seen the suicide alive, had left him very merry, and he remembered how strange he and the other jurors had thought that, at the time.
>
> Ch. 62

Like the figure of Death in Holbein's series, Dickens' "grotesque fantastic figure" disports himself in an incongruously merry dance which Dickens labels in his page heading, "Ominous Mirth." The dance is in Ralph's honor, a sign that Death has claimed him, for upon quitting the graveyard Ralph commits suicide, unlamented by anyone.

Mr. Merdle, the financier in *Little Dorrit,* also takes his own life, an event which, like Ralph Nickleby's suicide, is preceded by a Dance of Death, with the difference that Merdle himself appears to be dancing down the street.[9] Dancing to one's own funeral must be the height of grotesque inversion, and the warning couched in these macabre scenes is, of course, to so live one's life that such ultimate denials of one's humanity need not be contemplated.

Against these self-destructive figures the significance of Scrooge looms large. He might easily have gone the way of Anthony Chuzzlewit, Ralph Nickleby, and Merdle, but he is redeemed in time. The nocturnal visitations of the genial spirits of Christmas Past and Christmas Present soften his heart, but the spectral figure of Christmas Future terrifies him into a complete turnabout. The confrontation with finality has produced the salutary effect Dickens hoped to create in his readers.

Neither chivalrous nor sexist (depending on one's point of view), Dickens did not relegate the great sins only to the masculine species. Women's vanity is repeatedly satirized in a manner which emphasizes the seriousness of the vice, rather than presenting it as a mere peccadillo. *Bleak House* contains a key image drawn after Holbein which turns the preservation of personal appearance into a moral folly. "Carriages rattle, doors are battered at, the world exchanges calls; ancient charmers with skeleton throats, and peachy cheeks that have a rather ghastly bloom upon them seen by daylight, when indeed these fascinating creatures look like Death and the Lady fused together, dazzle the eyes of men" (Ch. 56). Like Holbein's "Empress," Dickens' image describes the social procession of high-class "charmers" whose appearance suggests the grotesque merger of Death with the Lady. As Holbein's woodcut serves to instruct his viewers that Death will summon all, regardless of wealth or splendor, so Dickens' image instructs his readers that members of high society cannot prolong their lives by cosmetics.

The origin of Dickens' image here has its popular side as well. "Death and the Lady" had long been a subject for balladeers, German as well as English.[10] The subject of grisly Death accosting an attractive lady had obvious visual appeal and was, indeed, often drawn by way of illustration to the ballad.

The image of Death and the Lady recurs in Dickens, but not always with reference to a female character. In *Martin Chuzzlewit*

Hans Holbein, "The Empress"

this figure characterizes a Yankee land agent. "The compound figure of Death and the Lady at the top of the old ballad was not divided with greater nicety, and hadn't halves more monstrously unlike each other, than the two profiles of Zephaniah Scadder" (Ch. 21). Dickens used the image, which he had evidently drawn from a music cover's adaptation of Holbein, to emphasize visually Scadder's extreme duplicity.[11] Scadder indeed functions as Death, conducting the unsuspecting to plots of land where they will almost certainly die. Martin Chuzzlewit and Mark Tapley leave Scadder for Eden on a river vessel which "might have been old Charon's boat, conveying melancholy shades to Judgment" (Ch. 23). Here our sympathy lies with Death's (Scadder's) intended victims, and we learn with them to inquire more closely into Edenic schemes of all kinds.

Some of Dickens' most vicious characters are described as Death incarnate. In *Little Dorrit* Miss Wade describes her seducer, Henry Gowan, as being "like the dressed-up Death in the Dutch series;[12] whatever figure he took upon his arm, whether it was youth or age, beauty or ugliness, whether he danced with it, sang with it, played with it, or prayed with it, he made it ghastly" (Bk. II, Ch. 21). Not content to denigrate Gowan through a single allusion, Dickens associates him with the Death figure in several of Holbein's plates: "The Empress" (whose "Figure" he seems to take "upon his arm"), "The Old Woman" (accompanying whom Death plays a wooden psalter), and "The Nun" (whose prayers he interrupts). Again our sympathy is with the victim, and our revulsion is directed toward the deceptively handsome artist who has made himself a grotesque through his mistreatment of others.

One of Dickens' most ghoulish characters, the lawyer Vholes, whose profession Dickens satirized in *Bleak House,* is also drawn in such a way as to suggest his affinities with the figure of Death. Esther recalls,

> "I never shall forget those two seated side by side in the lantern's light; Richard, all flush and fire and laughter, with the reins in his hand; Mr. Vholes, quite still, black-gloved, and buttoned up, looking at him as if he were looking at his prey and charming it. I have before me the whole picture of the warm dark night, the summer lightning, the dusty track of road closed in by hedgerows and high

trees, the gaunt pale horse with his ears pricked up, and the driving away at speed to Jarndyce and Jarndyce."

Ch. 37

Esther's description of "the whole picture" in some ways resembles Rowlandson, particularly "The Gig," and in other ways suggests Holbein, but it is also a painterly innovation on the traditional theme.[13] Rowlandsons's "Gig" shows a carriage overturning, spilling out a young couple while Death sits astride a tombstone. In Dickens' description Vholes, as Death, leads Richard away from Ada to his certain destruction. Vholes even assumes the attitude common to Death in Holbein's series, an intense concentration on "his prey" whose doom is sealed. Death does not *dance* away with his victim, but drives "away at speed."

The image of Death and the Lady is one of the principal means of satirizing Mrs. Skewton of *Dombey and Son,* whose vanity causes her to resist reality by personal deceptions which she believes effective in concealing her age. The description of her nocturnal preparations suggests Holbein's "Countess" who is assisted in attiring by a lady in waiting, and by Death, his hourglass set prominently in the foreground, but Dickens fuses the lady in waiting and Death into one character helping "Cleopatra" to disrobe:

Mrs. Skewton's maid appeared, according to custom, to prepare her gradually for night. At night, she should have been a skeleton, with dart and hour-glass, rather than a woman, this attendant; for her touch was as the touch of Death. The painted object shrivelled underneath her hand; the form collapsed, the hair dropped off, the arched dark eyebrows changed to scanty tufts of grey; the pale lips shrunk, the skin became cadaverous and loose; an old, worn, yellow, nodding woman, with red eyes, alone remained in Cleopatra's place, huddled up, like a slovenly bundle, in a greasy flannel gown.

Ch. 27

Other appearances of Mrs. Skewton reinforce the sense of connection to Holbein. Foolishly clinging to the demeanor and the designation of "Cleopatra" attributed to her in her youth, Mrs. Skewton reclines languidly in a barouche when taking the air, and is attended by "a tall, wan and thin" character whose name, Withers, suggests

Hans Holbein, "The Countess"

the touch of death. Picturesque satire and grotesque imagery here go hand in hand, bone in bone. Mrs. Skewton is the victim of her own picturesque pretensions. Living by a false, "pretty" image attributed to her years ago, she, like other victims of Death in the Dance, has no knowledge of his proximity, and persists in acting the coquette right up to the moment when Death claims her. "It was a tremendous sight to see this old woman in her finery leering and mincing at Death, and playing off her youthful tricks upon him as if he had been the Major" (Ch. 37). This image recalls, once again, Holbein's "Empress" strolling with Death on her arm. There is probably no image more forceful than the Dance of Death to express the futility of such intense self-deception. Yet, better to be the deceived than the deceiver. Better to be Death's unwitting fool than to be identified with Death himself.

The Dance of Death appears in recognizable, traditional form behind Mrs. Skewton, as it does behind her underworld counterpart, Mrs. Brown. Spying on Edith, Dombey's intended, Mrs. Brown appears in the guise of Death. "A withered and very ugly old woman... scrambled up from the ground—out of it, it almost appeared—and stood in the way. 'Let me tell your fortune, my pretty lady,' said the old woman, munching with her jaws, as if the Death's Head beneath her yellow skin were impatient to get out" (Ch. 27). Edith's fortune, as we already suspect, is not a pretty one, but only saints and demons enjoy such foreknowledge.

The two men who control Edith's fortune, Dombey and Carker, are described at critical junctures in their respective life and death by imagery which makes a highly inventive turn on the Dance of Death and makes that medieval tradition peculiarly meaningful in the industrial age. The figure of Death is transformed into an emblem of modern industrialized society, a train, which Dickens refers to repeatedly as "a type of the triumphant monster, Death." This transformation of the traditional into the modern is startling enough, but Dickens goes yet another step and makes the extended image illustrate the mind of the heartless industrialist. Mr. Dombey, his hopes for a son and heir crushed by the death of Paul, travels from London by train, but the journey is really into himself:

> Tortured by these thoughts he carried monotony with him, through the rushing landscape, and hurried headlong, not through a rich and

> varied country, but a wilderness of blighted plans and gnawing jealousies. The very speed at which the train was whirled along mocked the swift course of the young life that had been borne away so steadily and so inexorably to its foredoomed end. The power that forced itself upon its iron way—its own—defiant of all paths and roads, piercing through the heart of every obstacle, and dragging living creatures of all classes, ages, and degrees behind it, was a type of the triumphant monster, Death.
>
> Ch. 20

It is the old figure of Death from the old series, but updated to the age of the machine, a rich metaphor operating on multiple levels. The landscape rushing past the windows reflects the quality of Dombey's soul, a "wilderness of blighted plans and gnawing jealousies," while the movement of the train itself is likened to the inexorable rushing of Death. Dombey's life plans have been irrevocably altered by Death's seizure of his only son, an action visually represented by the rushing of the train, "defiant of all paths and roads, piercing through the heart of every obstacle." There is also the subtlest suggestion that Dombey, the victim, shares some of the characteristics of Death. His single-minded concentration on building a financial empire is, like Death's, "a power that forced itself upon its iron way." To accomplish his dreams of dynasty he has pitilessly ignored the useless daughter who cannot succeed to his business, and he enters into a loveless marriage in the vain hope of a male heir. He has, like Death, pierced "through the heart of every obstacle," and dragged living creatures behind him.

Having established Death as an unfeeling machine moving at ruthless speed, Dickens returns to this image late in the novel. Now Death is directed towards Carker, the nefarious schemer who has ruined Dombey's business and contributed to the destruction of his marriage. Carker finally realizes all is over for him when he feels the sensation of Death's presence, a moving presence similar to what Dombey has experienced. "Again that flight of Death came rushing up, again went on, impetuous and resistless, again was nothing but a horror in his mind, dark as the scene and undefined as its remotest verge" (Ch. 55). Because of the earlier image of Death which is so frequently repeated in this book, we see in Death's appearance to Carker not the traditional skeletal figure, but the form of an engine. Shortly thereafter Carker dies, fleeing from the vengeful Dombey, and the instrument of his death is what the imagery has foreshadowed: a train.

The frontispiece done by Phiz for the bound edition of the novel, unlike the cover for the monthly numbers, shows an engine in a prominent position. To the left of the central vignette of Florence and little Paul there appears an engine with rolling eyes bearing down upon the figure of a man. To the right of the central vignette is a traditional figure of death (and, rather unaccountably, since Dickens does not describe it, the devil) appearing to old Mrs. Skewton. Thus has Phiz combined the traditional with the non-traditional emblems of death, clearly reflecting Dickens' invention.

The image of the train as an updated engine of Death carries powerful moral connotations on the personal level, but Dickens makes this complex image function on a social level as well. To build the railroad, whole neighborhoods were ripped out of the earth, a phenomenon Dickens examines in Staggs Gardens. Human habitations simply cease to exist, as the instruments of industrialization place their mechanical mark where poor, but growing, gardens once flourished.

A certain ambiguity accompanies Dickens' description of the railroads. They were, after all, the most visible sign of the progress most Englishmen applauded, but the price for industrial progress is high. Its cost is, indeed, the death and displacement of many who might have muddled along in a pre-industrial era.

With this image of the train as something grotesque and ambiguously pernicious, we have moved beyond imagery related to a single artist or a single tradition. While Dickens clearly learned from Holbein and Hogarth how to visualize the grotesque reality beneath a sometimes deceptive surface, his own eye perceived in contemporary surroundings a wide range of grotesque possibilities. In three novels from different periods of his career (*The Old Curiosity Shop,* 1841; *Hard Times,* 1854; and *Great Expectations,* 1861), grotesquerie stems from somewhat different antecedents and carries moral meanings sweeping in their implications. Studying this imagery tells us a good deal about Dickens' altering moral perspective.

Chapter Four
The Grotesque Corrective

IN THE 1868 preface to *Martin Chuzzlewit* Dickens wrote,

> What is exaggeration to one class of minds and perceptions is plain truth to another. That which is commonly called a long-sight perceives in a prospect innumerable features and bearings non-existent to a short-sighted person. I sometimes ask myself whether there may occasionally be a difference of this kind between some writers and some readers: whether it is *always* the writer who colors highly, or whether it is now and then the reader whose eye for color is a little dull?

Again, in a late essay entitled "The Spirit of Fiction" Dickens carried on the defense of the writer as seer:

> Greater differences still exist between the common observer and the writer of genius. The former accuses the latter of intentional exaggeration, substitution, addition, and has never been able in society

> to see the startling phenomena which he condemns in the romance as melodramatic and unnatural. The reason is, that such an individual has never developed the sense required for the seeing such things.[1]

What Dickens sought to do was to help his readers develop "the sense required for the seeing such things," and, in order to help the reader see, he relies often on the grotesque.

Some of the people and places Dickens describes are so remote from the armchairs of his readers that he must employ startling images of incongruity if he is to awaken his readers to the reality of those lives. Grotesque imagery, as I have suggested earlier, carries a feeling of incongruity and of fear, for the world revealed to us is the one we inhabit, only seen from another perspective. We are not able to dismiss such images as fairytales, for they are grounded in reality. Nor are we able simply to laugh away these images as something propounded merely for our amusement. Comedy and grotesquerie may, and in Dickens they certainly do, mingle, but they are not the same. Wolfgang Kayser has made the interesting observation that "in the genuine grotesque the spectator becomes directly involved at some point where a specific meaning is attached to the event. In the humorous context, on the other hand, a certain distance is maintained throughout and, with it, a feeling of security and indifference."[2]

Dickens needed to have his readers involved, not indifferent, if reform were to occur, and while he is quite capable of merging didacticism with delight as his eighteenth-century predecessors did, his aim is a change in the hearts of his readers. The particular change he sought differs in each of the novels considered here (*The Old Curiosity Shop, Hard Times,* and *Great Expectations*), and the nature of the grotesque alters correspondingly. With extraordinary inventiveness Dickens shapes the grotesque to his varying purpose and, in so doing, shows us how visible—and how psychological a phenomenon it may be. He also reveals to us through his grotesque imagery his shifting perspective on the nineteenth-century world from one in which the reform of social structures seems possible to one in which the only reform that appears likely is that within the individual heart.

1. NATIONALIST NOSTALGIA: *THE OLD CURIOSITY SHOP*

Balancing the grotesque against an offsetting mode was part of Dickens' intention from the outset of *The Old Curiosity Shop.* In spite of the fact that this novel evolved in seemingly haphazard fashion, what Dickens said in his 1848 preface is largely borne out by his achievement:

> In writing this book, I had it always in my fancy to surround the lonely figure of the child with grotesque and wild, but not impossible, companions, and to gather about her innocent face and pure intentions, associates as strange and uncongenial as the grim objects that are about her bed when her history is first foreshadowed.

The idea of juxtaposing Nell with incongruous figures occurs to Master Humphrey at the beginning of the book: "It would be a curious speculation....to imagine her in her future life, holding her solitary way among a crowd of wild grotesque companions; the only pure, fresh, youthful object in the throng." Master Humphrey's curiosity, as well as the reader's, is increased by the image of her amid "heaps of fantastic things:"

> If these helps to my fancy had all been wanting, and I had been forced to imagine her in a common chamber, with nothing unusual or uncouth in its appearance, it is very probable that I should have been less impressed with her strange and solitary state. As it was, she seemed to exist in a kind of allegory.[3]

The suggestion of allegory arises from the juxtaposition of grotesquerie with neoclassical feminine beauty traceable to the works of Canova and Thorwaldsen that Dickens admired. Nell's ethereal purity has an otherworldly quality captured by Maclise in the final plate, a quality akin to that idealized spirituality Maclise had painted in "The Spirit of Chivalry." Her beauty is at once an ideal to aim for in this world and a quality better suited for the next one.

Nell's neoclassical fragility is juxtaposed with distorted characters and disorienting scenes that threaten her very survival. What Dickens achieves by this juxtaposition of neoclassicism and the grotesque is an allegory suggesting that modern industrialized society has lost the cohesiveness that once offered concern for its weakest, most vulnerable, yet most valuable beings. Whether or not the ideal world ever existed is unimportant. Dickens suggests what ought to exist, what English tradition might have evolved into, what ideal should have guided the nascent industrial nation. In place of a fragmented, increasingly materialistic society lacking the social structure to care for the vulnerable, there might have developed a society with the institutions to implement the Christian teachings observed only in platitudes rather than in deeds.

The use of the grotesque in this allegory is very much what Angus Fletcher suggested as a reformist possibility in any age. And the implicit message is very close to what A.W. Pugin, among others, perceived as a need for reform in mid-century England. Pugin's book *Contrasts* appeared in 1836, just five years prior to *The Old Curiosity Shop,* and it addressed a problem similar to the one Dickens considers in his novel. Pugin laments the falling-away from social cohesion that characterized the middle ages. His vision of a more nearly perfect earthly order is of a cathedral town dominated by soaring spires, unified by Gothic architecture emblematic of the flourishing in deed of the Christian spirit. In the famous first plate of the book, Pugin contrasts a Catholic town in 1440 with the same town in 1840. Gothic variety and unity have vanished behind a facade of dully functional buildings all too indicative of the mind-numbing activity carried on within. And if the curbed and regulated populace rebels, the New Jail occupying the former pleasure grounds, dominates the foreground and awaits the disillusioned.[4]

Protestant Dickens did not share Pugin's desire for a restoration of the Catholic establishment, but he did raise a similar question as to whether modern industrialization had not been purchased at the cost of destroying a past that was both aesthetically and spiritually satisfying. The question he raised, and the implicit answer that somehow the past had provided better for the poor, reflected widely shared views. E.R. Norman has observed about William Cobbett that "His romantic illusions about the social and charitable work for the poor performed by the medieval monasteries...reflected a popular notion."[5] The aura surrounding the Gothic, for Protestant and Catholic alike, carried the connotations of a better, more concerned and caring society.

The scenes Nell encounters frequently contain Gothic buildings in disrepair, emblematic representation of a nation whose spiritual life is in disarray. She and her grandfather first pause in a small ancient village whose church is "old and grey, with ivy clinging to the walls and around the porch... [with] low latticed windows [looking in upon] worm-eaten books...and baize of whitened-green mouldering from the pew sides.... Everything told of long use and quiet slow decay" (Ch. XVII).

Nell's final resting place is a Gothic structure "fast hastening to decay, empty and desolate" (Ch. XLVI). Two plates by George Cattermole, "A very Aged, Ghostly Place," and "Resting among the Tombs," capture the essence of Gothic decay. Dickens had enlisted the particular help of his friend Cattermole for this book, Cattermole having achieved some reputation for his drawing of antiquities. When the parts of the book had been completed, Dickens wrote Cattermole, "This is *the very first time* any designs for what I have written have touched and moved me, and caused me to feel that they expressed the idea I had in my mind."[6]

What Dickens appears to have had in mind here is a complex allegory touching deep national sentiments. His particular use of the Gothic is not happenstance. Other than in *The Mystery of Edwin Drood* his architectural description is generally more suggestive than particular. But his design in *The Old Curiosity Shop* necessitated description of the architectural style considered by his contemporaries indigenously English. The rebuilding of the Houses of Parliament in 1834 in Gothic rather than classical style is the clearest indicator of this preference. "Medievalism as a facet of patriotism was as much in the air as was Gothic as a facet of culture," Robert F. Jordan has claimed.[7]

Encouraged by the picturesque aesthetic, the Gothic Revival was at its height, its broken outlines, rough textures, and play of light and shadows capturing the essence of the picturesque.[8] When he describes Gothic architecture in *The Old Curiosity Shop,* Dickens plays to that taste, yet he does not create such settings merely for their visual and topical appeal, but for their allegorical suggestiveness. The Gothic architecture visited by Nell is in a ruined condition, enabling Dickens to call attention to the lamentable state of countless medieval buildings throughout England, and, more importantly, to suggest that such neglect may indicate a decline of interest in matters of the spirit.

A very Aged, Ghostly Place

George Cattermole, "A very aged, ghostly place"

Dickens extends his allegorical meaning considerably by making Nell a kind of modern pilgrim in the manner of John Bunyan's still widely read book. More than a neoclassical, vulnerable little figure finding Gothic decay instead of receiving spiritual sustenance, Nell becomes representative of the spiritual pilgrim wandering in a materialist age.

Nell and her grandfather are often designated "pilgrims." "The Pilgrimage Begins," reads Dickens' title for the illustration of Nell and her grandfather leaving London. "The Pilgrimage Renewed" reads the heading on a later page (Ch. XLIII). Pausing to rest in a country meadow outside London, Nell recalls that "there had been an old copy of the Pilgrim's Progress, with strange plates, upon a shelf at home, over which she had often pored whole evenings." She identifies their restful meadow with a place in Bunyan's book, and tells her grandfather, "I feel as if we were both Christian, and laid down on this grass all the cares and troubles we brought with us" (Ch. XV).

The neoclassical Nell's identification with Christian, and the Gothic settings furnish one pole in the novel, without which the world would seem given over, variously and entertainingly, yet ubiquitously, to the grotesque. Virtually all of the other characters are grotesques of one sort or another, and they whirl about the gentle Nell in a kaleidoscope of bewildering colors and shapes. Kit Nubbles is a comic grotesque, his exaggerated features rudely contrasted with Nell's perfection, but in a way which brings her delight rather than fear. His "uncommonly wide mouth, very red cheeks, [and] turned-up nose" gave him a "most comical expression of face" (Ch. 1). These features also give him an ingenuous appearance suitable to his fundamental honesty and loyalty, though his wide-awake expression does prefigure Mrs. Jarley's waxworks and the giant figure-head Quilp buys as a semblance of Kit. His features, like those of the figure-head, lack the complexity of those of most human beings, seeming to be reduced to a few simple lines, but the reduction is comic rather than satiric or diabolical.

The drunken and dirty Swiveller is also a grotesque, a being disinclined to exert the effort to maintain himself in any kind of order, yet a kindly and decent man capable of extending affection to the degree that another grotesque, the Marchioness, is saved from dingy despair.

Of all the grotesques in this book (and, I am tempted to say, in any other) Daniel Quilp is the most extraordinary. Boundlessly energetic, defiant of all conventions, the dwarf breaks enough categories to make one wonder whether he ought to be classified as human. One of Browne's illustrations shows him leaning out a window beside which a sign reads "Man Beast." Quilp is clearly both.

This practical-joke loving, irrepressible figure springs from certain affinities within his creator, but he also has certain pictorial antecedents. Fuseli's well-known and often reproduced "Nightmare" shows an impish incubus perched above the fainting figure of a neoclassical young woman. The basis of Dickens' plot may well derive from this grotesque-neoclassical juxtaposition, but in a specific scene he draws his own variant on this famous picture.[9]

Early in the book Quilp entertains his poor wife "with a succession of such horrible grimaces, as none but himself and nightmares had the power of assuming" (Ch. IV). Much later Quilp startles his wife into a faint by suddenly appearing when she had assumed he was dead. In this scene he is described as "looking at his insensible wife like a dismounted nightmare" (Ch. XLIX).

Resembling nightmare himself, Quilp fits right into a world of waxworks, of dwarfs and giants, and of puppeteers in churchyards. These forms that distort or mimic life are the forms of popular street art, as well as forms represented in graphic satire. What Dickens has used to carry part of his reformist message are the very arts available to the lowest class of English society. These arts do not offer up idealized impressions of human life. Rather, they capture antic gestures at frozen moments in a wide-awake, staring posture that startles by its semblance to reality. Mrs. Jarley says her "calm and classical" waxwork has

> a constantly unchanging air of coldness and gentility; and so like life, that if wax-work only spoke and walked about, you'd hardly know the difference. I won't go so far to say, that, as it is, I've seen wax-work quite like life, but I've certainly seen some life that was exactly like wax-work."
>
> Ch. XXVII

The resemblance between reality and its popular artistic representation is almost too close. To infuse these figures with life requires

Henry Fuseli, "The Nightmare," The Detroit Institute of Arts, Gift of Mr. and Mrs. Bert L. Smokler and Mr. and Mrs. Laurence A. Fleischman

only the animating imagination, a quality Nell brings to her odd resting place among them:

> She slept, for their better security, in the room where the wax-work figures were, and she never retired to this place at night but she tortured herself—she could not help it—with imagining a resemblance, in some one or other of their death-like faces, to the dwarf, and this fancy would sometimes so gain upon her that she would almost believe he had removed the figure and stood within the clothes. Then there were so many of them with their great glassy eyes—and, as they stood one behind the other all about her bed, they looked so like living creatures, and yet so unlike in their grim stillness and silence, that she had a kind of terror of them for their own sakes.
>
> Ch. XXIX

The close proximity between life and this art tells the viewer nothing about himself. Such art does not interpret or teach, but merely mimics, and in so doing, plays to the lowest of human emotions: curiosity.

Such intentionally representative art becomes totemic, inspiring fear in Nell, sadism in Quilp. Unable to take out his vengeance on Kit Nubbles, Quilp buys

> a great, goggle-eyed, blunt-nosed figure-head of some old ship.... It reached from floor to ceiling; and thrusting itself forward, with that excessively wide-awake aspect, and air of somewhat obtrusive politeness, by which figure-heads are usually characterized, seemed to reduce everything else to mere pigmy proportions.
>
> Ch. LXII

The demonic Quilp, beating the figure-head with an iron bar, cries out, "Is it like Kit—is it his picture, his image, his very self?" Quilp takes art for reality, releasing his hatred of the good Kit on a piece of popular art close enough to be "his picture."

While attacking this lifeless, yet too representational image, Quilp acts out the grotesque he is. He is like the animated wax-work or figure-head—a figure out of grotesque graphic satire—or out of medieval sculpture. At the old gate-way of the town where the wax-works are displayed, Nell encounters Quilp in a scene reminiscent of Gothic fiction:

> With a mingled sensation of curiosity and fear, she slowly approached the gate, and stood still to look up at it, wondering to see how dark, and grim, and cold, it looked.
>
> There was an empty niche from which some old statue had fallen or been carried away hundreds of years ago,
>
> Ch. XXVII

and from that very niche emerges the gargoyle shape of Quilp. Browne's illustration has aptly made Quilp look like a fallen gargoyle, but he is more than a medieval grotesque. Like that of his villainous predecessors in Gothic fiction his lascivious desire triggers sexual fear in the heroine. Yet the sexual dimensions of the novel are never expressed overtly in a manner to shock the age. By evoking the conventions of Gothic fiction and the grotesque, Dickens can suggest sexuality to the knowing, yet appear chastely correct to the rigidly repressed.[10]

Early in the novel Quilp asks the astonished little heroine, "How should you like to be my number two, Nelly?"

"To be what, sir?"

"My number two, Nelly; my second; my Mrs. Quilp," said the dwarf."

It is not inconceivable that the position will open up quite soon, for Mrs. Quilp clearly is being worried and frightened to death. Entering her party unexpectedly, Quilp threatens her with the animalistic remark, "If ever you listen to these beldames again, I'll bite you." Then he punishes her by forcing her to sit up with him all night while he smokes a glowing cigar. The weekly and the monthly numbers end with Quilp

> smoking and drinking in the same position, and staring listlessly out of the window with the dog-like smile always on his face, save when Mrs. Quilp made some involuntary movement of restlessness or fatigue; and then it expanded into a grin of delight.
>
> Ch. IV

To close the chapter, Browne has drawn a splendid little vignette of Mr. and Mrs. Quilp, she all timorous apprehension, and he tilted back in his chair with his cigar extended. The next chapter begins by drawing attention to that cigar still glowing with suggestively sexual potency.

Nell hides from Quilp

Hablot Browne, "Nell Hides from Quilp"

Everything that Quilp does is exaggerated beyond the normal limits. At the breakfast-table with his wife and mother-in-law,

> he by no means diminished the impression he had just produced, for he ate hard eggs, shell and all, devoured gigantic prawns with the heads and tails on, chewed tobacco and water-cresses at the same time and with extraordinary greediness, drank boiling tea without winking, bit his fork and spoon till they bent again, and in short performed so many horrifying and uncommon acts that the women were nearly frightened out of their wits and began to doubt if he were really a human creature.
>
> Ch. V

Outlandish, fiendishly energetic, and sexually threatening, Quilp is the quintessential grotesque, and, as such, not quite suitable for the normal world. But the world Quilp inhabits is not normal, if by normalcy we mean stability, predictability, and consonance of the past with the present. The grotesque Quilp is at ease in a world so filled with uncertainties that it is perhaps best described as amphibious. Belonging neither to land nor to the river, Quilp's wharf ambiguously occupies both, a fit symbol for a world in flux. Fitting, too, is the "amphibious boy" who attends Quilp and who is more comfortable standing on his head than on his feet. It is an inverted world that Quilp sardonically enjoys, and the fearsome possibility looms that this image of inversion prefigures the world to come.

Little Nell can find no resting place in such a world; she seems to require a quiet meadow in which Wordsworthian nature heals the spirit, but that landscape evocative of a simpler, more wholesome life, has passed away. The landscape of the present—and of the future—is closer to Quilp's "Wilderness," his recreational retreat.

This choice spot clearly inverts the picturesque, and its perverse proprietor revels in the discomforts it offers his guests. A summer house "in an advanced state of decay," with a "cracked and leaky roof," the Wilderness too literally embodies the epithets Quilp accords it. "You're fond of the beauties of nature," said Quilp with a grin. "Is this charming, Brass? Is it unusual, unsophisticated, primitive?" The obsequious Brass replies in the affirmative, underscoring his own suitability for the grotesque.

But who other than a grotesque would take tea with Quilp in the

Wilderness? Sally Brass, whose coupling with Quilp outside the covers of the novel is broadly hinted, bears an uncomfortable, category-blurring likeness to her brother:

> In face she bore a striking resemblance to her brother Sampson—so exact, indeed, was the likeness between them, that had it consorted with Miss Brass's maiden modesty and gentle womanhood to have assumed her brother's clothes in a frolic and sat down beside him, it would have been difficult for the oldest friend of the family to determine which was Sampson and which Sally, especially as the lady carried upon her upper lip certain reddish demonstrations, which, if the imagination had been assisted by her attire, might have been mistaken for a beard.
>
> Ch. XXXIII

Androgyny may be the wave of the future, but Dickens associates it here and in the Murdstones of *David Copperfield* with the grotesque. His ideal of femininity remains nostalgically close to neoclassicism.[11]

The industrial, material thrust of the changing society seems in *The Old Curiosity Shop* to be turning many into grotesques. The new industrialism forces men to act like giants, to work in situations scarcely human:

> In a large and lofty building, supported by pillars of iron, with great black apertures in the upper walls, open to the external air; echoing to the roof with the beating of hammers and roar of furnaces, mingled with the hissing of red-hot metal plunged in water, and a hundred strange unearthly noises never heard elsewhere; in this gloomy place, moving like demons among the flame and smoke, dimly and fitfully seen, flushed and tormented by the burning fires, and wielding great weapons, a faulty blow from any one of which must have crushed some workman's skull, a number of men laboured like giants.
>
> Ch. XLIV

Both the work and the "Wilderness" of this changing society require the participants to transform themselves into something less than human. This flotsam-jetsam world of random chaos ultimately claims Quilp, and our last sight of him is of a thing, a human being reduced to a bit of tidal refuse:

> [The water] toyed and sported with its ghastly freight, now bruising it against the slimy piles, now hiding it in mud or long rank grass, now dragging it heavily over rough stones and gravel, now feigning to yield it to its own element, and in the same action luring it away, until tired of the ugly plaything, it flung it on a swamp—a dismal place where pirates had swung in chains, through many a wintry night—and left it there to bleach.
>
> Ch. LXVII

The amphibious world has claimed Quilp for its own, and he ends in a macabre mixture of swamp and slime, a suitably distorted, inhuman ending for one so intent on making himself thoroughly grotesque.

But neither does Nell survive. Her end, by contrast to Quilp's, is a deeply spiritual one. Her spirit passes quietly, but mournfully, from a world which seems no longer to have a house for her. The Gothic ruins surrounding her offer her only the solace of knowing that death comes to all.

Her death occasioned an enormous outpouring of grief,[12] but it was not just the death of a fair little creature that was lamented. She represented something of goodness, some opportunity missed, something absent from a social structure inadequate to assist her like. She was a lovely anomaly in a world where work has lost its dignity and leisure no longer provides renewal. The world seems given over to the grotesque with but a nostalgic reminder of what was.

The survivors are the kindly grotesques Kit, Dick Swiveller, and the Marchioness, together with those anomalous and aging figures from another era, Mr. and Mrs. Garland and Mr. Abel. These maimed and distorted figures will make their way through the amphibious world, but without the company of the idealized little Nell.

What Dickens conveyed here was the sense, widely-held, that somehow modern progress and industrialization were carrying England away from its better traditions—that the caring spirit suggested by the Gothic, or English, style, and the purity of neoclassicism had given way to a hodgepodge of grotesque images deeply indicative of the chaotic values or loss of values apparently ascendant.[13]

2. CONTEMPORARY REALISM: *HARD TIMES*

Hard Times is a moral tract for the times, unrelievedly immersed in the present, and unswervingly insistent that grotesquerie is the visual

George Cattermole, "Resting among the Tombs"

corollary of certain attitudes ascendant in the industrializing world. The grotesque imagery in *Hard Times* comes from graphic satire, from cartoon caricature using few, but telling, lines. Swift and keen, the satirical thrust in *Hard Times* arises from the near perfect conjunction of the spare elements of the visual image and the spare syntax of the prose.

Whereas *The Old Curiosity Shop* contains many scenes of the Gothic picturesque, evidence of earlier architecture or gentle picturesque landscapes has disappeared from the world of *Hard Times.* Nature, not just the picturesque impression of it, but nature itself has been all but obliterated by man's insensitive structures obscuring the earth. Early in the novel Stephen Blackpool wanders through the realm of his imagination and returns to reality. "The wind was blowing again, the rain was beating on the housetops, and the larger spaces through which he had strayed contracted to the four walls of his room" (Bk. I, Ch. 13). Even that lingering remnant of imagination that gives him restricted access to "the larger spaces" is being systematically destroyed by utilitarian educators, and what remains is indeed "contracted to the four walls of his room."

The outer world is dominated by the factory and its effects, so that even the moon, that most picturesque light, casts only "shadows of the steam-engines at rest" (Bk. I, Ch. 10). Only when Stephen falls into a pit can he look out, from his severely restricted vantage point, upon an unimpeded view of the stars—and that unveiled view into the heavens foreshadows his death.

Those whose education and affluence could enable them to enjoy the delights of the imagination and the natural world have blinded themselves to all but mathematical exactness. Gradgrind's Stone Lodge, for instance, is "situated on a moor," but no curving picturesque landscaping alleviates the starkness implicit in its very name. "A lawn and garden and an infant avenue, all ruled straight like a botanical account-book" grace the dwelling, and make for the antithesis of the pleasing picturesque (Bk. I, Ch. 3).

Neither cultivated nor uncultivated nature suggests the picturesque. Bounderby relishes the growing of cabbages in his once picturesque garden. Mrs. Sparsit, spying on Jem Harthouse and Louisa one miserable night, experiences the natural world at its least Edenic, most grotesque. "She thought of the wood, and stole towards it, heedless of long grass and briers: of worms, snails and slugs, and all the creeping things that be" (Bk. II, Ch. 11). Like a snake in the grass she merges with this unpleasant environment occupied by standard denizens of the grotesque.

Although much has been made of Dickens' supposed lack of understanding of utilitarianism, political economy and laissez-faire economics, this criticism ultimately misses the point, for his satire was not directed against any of these particular attitudes.[14] He uses the terms current in contemporary discussion to underscore his interest in the present, but his moral concern is directed more broadly.

The moral reform Dickens seeks involves the particular value-carrying institutions of education (then in the hands of utilitarians)[15] and religion. He rightfully perceived that these institutions needed reformation, but his concern runs to the deep currents underlying society. *Hard Times,* in hortatory fashion, seeks to turn the English away from accepting a too limited view of human life, and its message is as pertinent today as it was then.

To Charles Knight, Dickens wrote, "My satire is against those who see figures and averages, and nothing else—the representatives of the wickedest and most enormous vice of this time—the men who, through long years to come, will do more to damage the real useful truths of political economy than I could do (if I tried) in my whole life."[16]

"Men who see figures and averages, and nothing else" are not necessarily political economists. Dickens makes clear in this letter, and elsewhere, that he respected much of the effort undertaken by that group. Dickens has grounded his satire explicitly in the period—but his concerns are not restricted to that period only. He wanted, as he wrote Carlyle, to "shake some people in a terrible mistake of these days."[17] The mistake persisting, the satire is equally apt, and *Hard Times* should be read not as a period piece, but as a book using a particularized setting to discuss a lamentably enduring problem.

The Old Curiosity Shop creates with an abundant prose style a cluttered world where discordant heaps of curiosities reflect the divergent characters unaccountably thrust together. By contrast, the spare world of *Hard Times* is a compulsively tidy world ordered on a pair of bare principles: that material fact is of primary importance, and that human beings are primarily interested in themselves, i.e., their material gain. Both principles narrow the range of human possibilities and emphasize the thingness of human life rather than the spiritual dimension. This reduction of life to such paltry dimensions, this willful shriveling of the spirit is fundamentally grotesque.

Thomas Gradgrind opens the novel with an abrupt annunciation of the first principle:

> "Now, what I want is Facts. Teach these boys and girls nothing but Facts. Facts alone are wanted in life. Plant nothing else, and root out everything else. You can only form the minds of reasoning animals upon Facts; nothing else will ever be of any service to them. This is the principle on which I bring up my own children, and this is the principle on which I bring up these children. Stick to Facts, sir!"

Coketown's stifling environment, so unpropitious to the flowering of the human spirit, is the embodiment of the demand for facts and only facts:

> Coketown...was a triumph of fact.... The jail might have been the infirmary, the infirmary might have been the jail, the townhall might have been either, or both, or anything else, for anything that appeared to the contrary in the graces of their construction. Fact, fact, fact, everywhere in the material aspect of the town; fact, fact, fact, everywhere in the immaterial.
>
> Bk. I, Ch. 5

The first principle is reasserted at the beginning of Chapter Eight, which is titled, "Never Wonder":

> Louisa had been overheard to begin a conversation with her brother one day, by saying "Tom, I wonder"—upon which Mr. Gradgrind, who was the person overhearing, stepped forth into the light and said, "Louisa, never wonder!"
>
> Herein lay the spring of the mechanical art and mystery of educating the reason without stooping to the cultivation of the sentiments and affections. Never wonder. By means of addition, subtraction, multiplication, and division, settle everything somehow, and never wonder.

Gradgrind's systematic suppression of wonder anticipates Mrs. General's shaping of a social character impervious to emotion in *Little Dorrit.*

The other dominant principle sounded throughout *Hard Times* is self-interest, a principle most succinctly expressed by James Harthouse: "Every man is selfish in everything he does, and I am exactly like the rest of my fellow-creatures" (Bk. II, Ch. 7).

Dickens takes these principles, these hard facts of life, as oft-expressed and as zealously held in our time as in his, and shows us the consequences of a life regulated in such wise. The somewhat abstract, and decidedly spare aspect of the book results from his making the characters essentially what they espouse.

Illustrations would have been superfluous in this novel, for Dickens has adopted the technique of his illustrators, themselves trained in a tradition of graphic satire extending back through Gillray and Rowlandson to Hogarth.[18] Like the graphic satirist, Dickens has made the most characteristic physical feature express the essential idea of the character. It is a technique he uses elsewhere—especially for minor characters—but nowhere else does he press the technique further. And nowhere else would it work so well; for these leading citizens insist on regulating their lives by certain rigid principles.

Gradgrind is introduced to us first through his peroration on fact because those words express what he is. No novelist has made his character more visually expressive of his own words than Dickens has made Gradgrind:

> The speaker's square forefinger emphasized his observations by underscoring every sentence with a line on the schoolmaster's sleeve. The emphasis was helped by the speaker's square wall of a forehead, which had his eyebrows for its base, while his eyes found commodious cellarage in two dark caves, overshadowed by the wall.... The speaker's obstinate carriage, square coat, square legs, square shoulders—nay, his very neckcloth, trained to take him by the throat with an unaccommodating grasp, like a stubborn fact, as it was—all helped the emphasis.

This "man of facts and calculations" wants to be presented as a man of no nonsense, but he is, in fact, presented to us as something almost nonsensically inhuman, a geometric figure whose "squareness" carries considerably more connotations than modern slang allows. So rigidly does he adhere to his precious facts that all softening influences on his character or his physiognomy have been rejected. Though we feel revulsion watching the effect of his rigid theory work its way on the young, we feel pathos at the end, for he has, with the best, albeit benighted, will in the world, reduced himself, his family, and his students to something below their human promise by battering them with his principles. In becoming so blatantly what he preaches, he has made himself, and all around him, grotesque.

Gradgrind's star pupil, Bitzer, is a prime example. Bitzer's mastery of "hard facts" equips him admirably for a life of cynical self-interest. He is emblematic of the sort who get ahead in the industrial society. Pallid, plodding, methodical, Bitzer hasn't even enough substance for the sun to rest on him:

> ...Sissy, being at the corner of a row on the sunny side, came in for the beginning of a sunbeam, of which Bitzer, being at the corner of a row on the other side...caught the end. But, whereas the girl was so dark-eyed and dark-haired that she seemed to receive a deeper and more lustrous colour from the sun, when it shone upon her, the boy was so light-eyed and light-haired that the self-same rays appeared to draw out of him what little colour he ever possessed.
>
> Bk. I, Ch. 2

The knowledgeable sun rests fully on Sissy Jupe, though she is demonstrably unsuited for Gradgrindian education in Political Economy. To the question, "What is the first principle of this science?" she returns "the absurd answer, 'To do unto others as I would that they should do unto me.'" Bitzer, the prematurely practical, knows better, and at the end he demonstrates how well he has been taught that

> the whole social system is a question of self-interest. What you must always appeal to, is a person's self-interest. It's your only hold. We are so constituted. I was brought up in that catechism when I was very young, Sir, as you are aware.

Gradgrind is caught in a trap of his own making. He cannot persuade his star pupil to act charitably in order to save Tom, for Bitzer's "catechism" did not include charity:

> It was a fundamental principle of the Gradgrind philosophy that everything was to be paid for. Nobody was ever on any account to give anybody anything, or render anybody help without purchase. Gratitude was to be abolished, and the virtues springing from it were

> not to be. Every inch of the existence of mankind, from birth to death, was to be a bargain across a counter. And if we didn't get to Heaven that way, it was not a politico economical place, and we had no business there.
>
> Bk. III, Ch. 8

Young Tom, whose life, if not his soul, is saved at the end in spite of Bitzer's calculated rule-playing, has grown into a sullen youth. Even as a child he chose, in true grotesque fashion, an animal rather than human image of himself. "I am a Donkey, that's what I am. I am as obstinate as one, I am more stupid than one, I get as much pleasure as one, and I should like to kick like one" (Bk. I, Ch. 8). His most passionate outburst is seen in his declaration, "I am sick of my life," and in his description of his parental roof as "this–jolly old–Jaundiced Jail."

Deprived of everything that might nourish one, Tom seems to grow up without a soul. His factual education leads him to believe in nothing but material pleasure, and he becomes a nondescript physical surface, whose grasping at pleasures only illustrates the hedonistic fallacy. By the end this disgraced "model child" is no more than the assumed surface of a clown:

> The father buried his face in his hands, and the son stood in his disgraceful grotesqueness, biting straw; his hands, with the black partly worn away inside, looking like the hands of a monkey. The evening was fast closing in and from time to time, he turned the whites of his eyes restlessly and impatiently towards his father. They were the only parts of his face that showed any life or expression, the pigment upon it was so thick.
>
> Bk. III, Ch. 7

Tom no longer has any self to express. His callous selfishness has encrusted his moral being just as clown paint covers his skin. He is no longer anything but a borrowed costume. To his sorrow, and to his credit, Gradgrind recognizes the grotesque creature he has made, a creature retaining only the slightest human animation. He is all too like the dying clown in *The Pickwick Papers,* a figure grotesquely marked by Death.

Louisa is bartered off to the highest bidder by this father who thinks that in making the greatest decision of her life, "it is not unimportant to take into account the statistics of marriage" (Bk. I,

Ch. 15). Even little Nell had more protection than that. Louisa returns home in disgrace, a renegade wife who places the blame for her life's failure where it belongs. When she enters her father's study, he is busy "proving something no doubt—probably, in the main, that the Good Samaritan was a Bad Economist." The child-woman, raised in disregard of the spirit's teaching, asks her mentor,

> "How could you give me life, and take from me all the inappreciable things that raise it from the state of conscious death? Where are the graces of my soul? Where are the sentiments of my heart? What have you done, O father, what have you done, with the garden that should have bloomed once, in this great wilderness here?"
>
> Bk. II, Ch. 12

An immaterial entity it may be, yet, as Dickens shows, the soul holds the key to whether life continues at all. Neglected or destroyed, the shrunken soul throws up a grotesque surface.

Dickens' admonitions regarding the education of the young remain quite as pertinent today as in 1854. His observations concerning the other value-carrying institution, the church, are more topical. He shows us a society that has provided buildings for religion, but not a people that spends much time within them. The visual satire suggests that popular disinterest may be owing partly to the uninviting, utilitarian aspect of those buildings:

> You saw nothing in Coketown but what was severely workful. If the members of a religious persuasion built a chapel there—as the members of eighteen religious persuasions had done—they made it a pious warehouse of red brick, with sometimes (but this is only in highly ornamented examples) a bell in a birdcage on the top of it. The solitary exception was the New Church; a stuccoed edifice with a square steeple over the door, terminating in four short pinnacles like florid wooden legs.
>
> Bk. I, Ch. 5

The "New Church" undoubtedly refers to one of the "Commissioners' Churches" built throughout England during the early part of the century. Ill-conceived attempts to woo the working masses back to the Established Church, these new churches were vaguely and cheaply "Gothic" in character. Those "four short pinnacles" are Coketown's miserly attempt at "Gothic" ornamentation.

In 1818 the Church Building Act had been passed, resulting eventually in the building of 214 churches.[19] Some of them evinced good design, but economy prevailed over aesthetics, leading Sir Kenneth Clark to assess the results as "perhaps the most completely unattractive architectural style ever employed."[20] John Summerson says, "The 'Commissioners' Churches' vary greatly in style and much more so in quality, but are almost always recognizable. There is a peculiar drabness about them, a slackness in the proportions, a lack of vitality, as if their designers had driven themselves to a task for which they had no heart."[21]

In providing Coketown with one of these Commissioners' churches, Dickens was not only adding a note of contemporary authenticity, he was also stressing architectural paucity and monotony that was patently grotesque. And that reflected the sorry state of the spiritual life in urban England.

Pugin had observed the same phenomenon, and had lamented the contemporary crudity of church building:

> It is not incumbent on all men to raise vast and splendid churches; but it *is* incumbent on all men to render the buildings they raise for religious purposes *more vast and beautiful than those in which they dwell.* This is all I contend for; but this is a feeling nearly if not altogether extinct. Churches are now built without the least regard to tradition, to mystical reasons, or even common propriety. A room full of seats at the least possible cost is the present idea of a church; and if any ornament is indulged in, it is a mere screen to catch the eye of the passerby, which is a most contemptible deception to hide the meanness of the real building.[22]

Coketown's churches epitomize Pugin's observation. Nothing distinguishes them from any other building, save a ludicrous "bird-cage," an ornament expressive only of impoverished ingenuity. Few of Coketown's inhabitants appear to frequent church or chapel. The only ones we see are Stephen and Rachel, characters whose inexplicable goodness has perplexed many of Dickens' critics. It is much easier to imagine them as spiritually misshapen in an environment so grotesque, yet there they are, offering a pure spiritual balance to this heavily materialistic society.

A recent book, *Church and Society in England 1770–1970* by E.R. Norman, substantiates the impression of the working-class that Dickens has given us. "Working-class men and women were not irreligious, though middle-class churchmen did not usually appreciate this, not having adequate tests by which to identify the nature of working-class religiosity."[23] Stephen's vow not to join the union was not a scabrous act of defiance, but a promise given Rachel in keeping with their religious beliefs. But even more indicative of the quiet workings of spiritual concerns in these two people is the special, deeply affectionate relationship they maintain even though they are prohibited from marrying each other.

In some mysterious fashion not yet understood by historians or sociologists, working-class people retained a sense of the spiritual. And that spiritual sense made itself felt in English society. "The religious sense of working men penetrated the early Labour movement. It combined with self-help doctrines to give English popular thought its most characteristic moralistic qualities. But it found no real home in the Churches."[24]

This deeply moral-spiritual and affectionate nature exemplified by Stephen and Rachel is found in the members of Sleary's Circus, who also contribute to the balancing element in *Hard Times.* All of these characters who show us that a life of more than hard fact is yet possible live on the fringes of society, whereas the leaders of the industrial town have formed themselves into misshapen, distorted creatures so far from radiant humanity as to be grotesque.

Josiah Bounderby reigns as king of the grotesques. He prides himself on being a self-made man, the pinnacle of Coketown society. "He was a rich man: banker, merchant, manufacturer, and what not" (Bk. I, Ch. 4). But the self that Bounderby has made and that he proclaims endlessly is in fact grotesque. He, too, is described initially with the swift strokes of the cartoonist like a big, round balloon—visibly expressive of the windbag he is:

> A man made out of a coarse material, which seemed to have been stretched to make so much of him. A man with a great puffed head and forehead, swelled veins in his temples, and such a strained skin to his face that it seemed to hold his eyes open, and lift his eyebrows up. A man with a pervading appearance on him of being inflated like a balloon, and ready to start.
>
> Bk. I, Ch. 4

As we smile at a cartoon, we smile at Bounderby. So boisterously, exuberantly does Dickens present him that we cannot help being amused—even while recognizing his abuse of power. To read *Hard Times* as merely "serious"[25] is to miss the mixture grotesquerie affords. Even the wretched marriage between Bounderby and Louisa, in many ways like Quilp's marriage, has its funny aspects. Bounderby's wedding speech, full of bombast and ludicrous overemphasis on calling a thing by its proper name, is a marvelous comic moment:

> "Ladies and gentlemen, I am Josiah Bounderby of Coketown. Since you have done my wife and myself the honour of drinking our healths and happiness, I suppose I must acknowledge the same; though, as you all know me, and know what I am, and what my extraction was, you won't expect a speech from a man who, when he sees a Post, says 'that's a Post,' and when he sees a Pump, says 'that's a Pump, and is not to be got to call a Post a Pump, or a Pump a Post, or either of them a Toothpick."
>
> Bk. I, Ch. 16

One cannot, without appearing ludicrous, pretend to be a plain-spoken man unless one has something plainly to say. Bounderby has not taken enough pains to acquire even elemental ideas about anything at all. He exults in his low origins and willfully neglects any of the gentler graces available to him through his wealth. No one could persuade him that the arts could have any positive impact on his life. "He delighted to live, barrack-fashion, among the elegant furniture, and he bullied the very pictures with his origin," refusing to give this costly ornamentation more than a nod of the head (Bk. II, Ch. 7).

With shrewd insight, Dickens shows us how upper class interests that might have been expected to defend the arts, join with this heinous philistinism of the resolutely bourgeois:

> The Gradgrind party wanted assistance in cutting the throats of the graces. They went about recruiting; and where could they enlist recruits more hopefully, than among the fine gentlemen who, having found out everything to be worth nothing, were equally ready for anything?
>
> Bk. II, Ch. 2

The thoroughly jaded, like Jem Harthouse, no longer take any interest in anything, save, perhaps, destroying whatever capacity to charity that remains among those they touch. Jem's destructive power connects with Bounderby's. And woe betide their hapless victims.

Bounderby's utter failure to understand the workers, a failure related to his abysmal ignorance of himself, leads him to make disastrous decisions on their behalf. Capable of thinking only in stereotypes, he is convinced that the workers really want to eat turtle soup with gold spoons. He is as sure as Bitzer, who expresses the idea, that "What one person can do, another can do;" thus the workers' failure to succeed as Bounderby has must be laid to their own laziness. And as to any need for recreation, well, they haven't any. "'As to their wanting recreations, ma'am,' said Bitzer, 'It's stuff and nonsense. I don't want recreations. I never did, and I never shall; I don't like 'em!'" (Bk. II, Ch. 1).

Dickens is not just showing us these hard facts types to ridicule and laugh at. Their demeanor may be humorously contemptible, but their actions may bring about the destruction of society as we have known it. And Dickens pleads with us, at a higher hortatory level than he generally uses, to heed the warning signals before it is too late:

> Utilitarian economists, skeletons of schoolmasters, Commissioners of Fact, genteel and used-up infidels, gabblers of many little dog's-eared creeds, the poor you will have always with you. Cultivate in them, while there is yet time, the utmost graces of the fancies and affections, to adorn their lives so much in need of ornament; or, in the day of your triumph, when romance is utterly driven out of their souls, and they and a bare existence stand face to face, Reality will take a wolfish turn, and make an end of you.
>
> Bk. II, Ch. 6

The reality Dickens speaks of here is in fact grotesquerie. Pressed beyond their human limits by principles better worked out on geometric surfaces, the people will act in the way they have been trained to act—even though it is not the way their trainers had intended. Dickens here acknowledges the union of the aesthetic and the moral. Like Ruskin he believes that a developed capacity to enjoy art is necessarily linked to the social virtues of dignity and restraint.

The world of Coketown is the industrial town without the contrast of *The Old Curiosity Shop*—not even a crumbling Gothic edifice.

Singlemindedly devoted to the utilitarian needs of the factory, the grotesquerie of Coketown cannot help warping the townspeople into grotesques as well:

> It was a town of red brick, or of brick that would have been red if the smoke and ashes had allowed it; but as matters stood it was a town of unnatural red and black like the painted face of a savage. It was a town of machinery and tall chimneys, out of which interminable serpents of smoke trailed themselves for ever and ever, and never got uncoiled. It had a black canal in it, and a river that ran purple with ill-smelling dye, and vast piles of buildings full of windows where there was a rattling and a trembling all day long, and where the piston of the steam-engine worked monotonously up and down like the head of an elephant in a state of melancholy madness. It contained several large streets all very like one another, and many small streets still more like one another, inhabited by people equally like one another, who all went in and out at the same hours, with the same sound upon the same pavements, to do the same work, and to whom every day was the same as yesterday and to-morrow, and every year the counterpart of the last and the next.
>
> Bk. I, Ch. 5

This is the grotesquerie of the modern world, the mind-numbing monotony of repetitive forms that lead to a surrealistic sort of madness. Ironically, the few touches of "fancy" Dickens uses to describe this industrial horror ("like the painted face of a savage;" "like the head of an elephant in a state of melancholy madness") would disappear from usage under the utilitarian scheme of education.

Yet there are reformable institutions here, and Dickens' letters written at this time indicate his continued belief that these social ills could be corrected. Although from our twentieth-century perspective *Hard Times* may seem to foreshadow the dreariness of the modern industrial landscape, Dickens seems still to feel that we can prevent ourselves from becoming grotesques. In *Great Expectations* that possibility is precluded by a poignant acceptance of the harsh fact that the modern world has made us all, to some degree, grotesque. Modern materialism seems to have so encouraged self-aggrandizement and so diminished compassion and fellow-feeling that our essential humanity has become distorted into grotesquerie. The sad recognition of this unhappy change lies at the heart of *Great Expectations.*

3. MYTHIC FUTURE: *GREAT EXPECTATIONS*

Great Expectations from the outset urges that one recognize the limitations inherent in the social order and adapt to them. It is not the inspiriting notion that sets *Nicholas Nickleby* attacking wretched schools or that moves *Dombey and Son* toward exposing the harmful callousness of the new industrial mentality. *Great Expectations* is suffused with the melancholy resignation that one must accept the world for what it is, and must try not to establish foolish fictions in front of reality.

The grotesque imagery here is more richly symbolic, operating not on an external, overt manner as in *The Old Curiosity Shop*—but on an internal plane that convinces us grotesquerie is inherent in modern society, and even in ourselves.

The emphasis in *Great Expectations* is not on the contrast between the grotesque and the non-grotesque, but on the recognition of inescapable grotesquerie in a changing world. Pip's growing awareness in this *bildungsroman* is of a self deeply suffused with the grotesque rather than a self distinctly separate from it. Part of the power of *Great Expectations* to move us so deeply lies in our recognition of Pip's growth as resembling our own.[26]

Pip begins his narration by recalling his earliest memory—a day on which he was, significantly, turned upside down. The convict's action is so swift, and Pip's young understanding so imperfect that he thinks the world has moved rather than he. "When the church came to itself—for he was so sudden and strong that he made it go head over heels before me, and I saw the steeple under my feet—when the church came to itself, I say, I was seated on a high tombstone."[27] Pip's maturation involves learning about inversions,[28] that things are not always what they seem, that the solutions to perplexing situations must be sought in himself rather than the world outside. But that lesson comes slowly and with pain.

Magwitch, who inverts the world first physically and later psychologically for Pip, presents himself initally as a traditional grotesque. He threatens Pip with inhuman, cannibalistic possibilities that recall the words of Daniel Quilp. " 'You fail, or you go from my words in any partickler, no matter how small it is, and your heart and your liver shall be tore out, roasted and ate.' " He identifies himself with the slimy animals that live on the marshes. " 'I wish I was a frog. Or a eel!'" And, as if these category mergers between cannibal and civilized, animal and human, were not enough, he appears to hover uncertainly between the living and the dead. "He looked in my young eyes as if he were eluding the hands of the dead people, stretching up cautiously out of their graves, to get a twist upon his ankle and pull him in."

Yet even the young Pip can recognize the essential humanity of Magwitch beneath his external grotesquerie. The child knows instinctively that he is not what he seems, and he learns from watching Joe that genuine compassion does not respond only to a properly presented surface.

The confrontation with the convict tinges the surrounding landscape with suggestions of restriction, even of prison bars rather than the open spaces we might normally associate with the psychology of a child or the physiography of a seascape:

> The marshes were just a long black horizontal line then, as I stopped to look after him; and the river was just another horizontal line, not nearly so broad nor yet so black; and the sky was just a row of long angry red lines and dense black lines intermixed.

Pip's repeated phrase, "just a...," could be the child's offhand manner of describing the familiar; or it could emphasize a restrictive quality quite at odds not only with the title but with our stereotype of what land so near the open sea should suggest. Whatever else that marsh landscape may mean, it does not herald great expectations of anything.

With blurred brush strokes abstractly evocative of the late Turner, Dickens paints a scene dominated by colors violently "intermixed" or meshed. The word "meshes" was "always used...for marshes in our country," Pip tells us in the next chapter. Given the context, we are likely to read "meshes" as a kind of trap, like the robe Clytemnestra had woven for Agamemnon. But our understanding of this word alters by the end of the book. The reader's perceptions change along with Pip's.

Early in the novel Pip's expectations are only that he will forever inhabit "the meshes" as Joe's assistant at the forge. Although such a life is not welcomed enthusiastically, Pip quietly accepts his lot until he encounters another kind of life in Satis House. His first perception of that house and of its strange proprietress was of grotesquerie, of a disturbing and failed attempt to halt the progress of time:

> I saw that everything within my view which ought to be white, had been white long ago, and had lost its lustre, and was faded and yellow. I saw that the bride within the bridal dress had withered like the dress, and like the flowers, and had no brightness left but the brightness of her sunken eyes. I saw that the dress had been put upon the rounded figure of a young woman, and that the figure upon which it now hung loose, had shrunk to skin and bone. Once, I had been taken to see some ghastly waxwork at the Fair, representing I know not what impossible personage lying in state. Once, I had been taken to one of our old marsh churches to see a skeleton in the ashes of a rich dress, that had been dug out of a vault under the church pavement. Now, waxwork and skeleton seemed to have dark eyes that moved and looked at me.
>
> Ch. 8

The figure of Miss Havisham makes young Pip want to cry out, while at the same time his early awareness of grotesquerie is confusedly mixed with his stunned observation of splendor. When he is asked by his sister to describe what he has seen, he cannot resist the temptation to fantasize, convinced as he is that no one will understand him if he tells what he has really seen. Though he willfully embellishes Satis House for Mrs. Gargery and Pumblechook, an act for which he later repents to Joe, Pip cannot resist the pernicious effects of that environment on his own image of himself. Under that unhealthy spell he adopts the inverted view that what he has experienced at Satis House is not grotesque, but picturesque. "Miss Havisham and Estella and the strange house and the strange life appeared to have something to do with everything that was picturesque" (Ch. 15). An attraction to the picturesque, as we have seen above, means a deeply troubled perceiver. And so Pip is at this stage, patterning his life upon the chimerical principles of the picturesque.

Under the spell of Miss Havisham and, especially Estella, Pip learns dissatisfaction. He comes to regard his old life as common—meaning, at this point, contemptible, though "common," like "meshes," undergoes a considerable alteration in meaning. By teaching him to regard himself as common Miss Havisham and Estella invert Pip's early world.

Only when Pip is forced to set aside his own fantasies concerning Estella and to recognize Miss Havisham's obsessive desire to use her ward as an instrument of vengeance, does he begin to realize the extent to which they have damaged him. Only then does he begin to speak knowingly of himself as a grotesque, first as a machine rather than human:

> Miss Havisham's intentions towards me, all a mere dream; Estella not designed for me; I only suffered in Satis House as a convenience, a sting for the greedy relations, a model with a mechanical heart to practice on when no other practice was at hand.
>
> Ch. 39

He returns to visit Miss Havisham, to let her know how he has suffered, and he then sees Satis House as representative of his own unhappily altered state. "With all that ruin at my feet and about me, it seemed a natural place for me, that day" (Ch. 44). Pip's changing perception of Satis House marks out stages in his own perception of himself, a self that he comes to see as partaking in, rather than contrasting with, the grotesque.

Pip's suffering and his severely reduced expectations do not embitter him, but increase his empathy. His final visit to Miss Havisham finds him "compassionating her, and thinking how in the progress of time I too had come to be a part of the wrecked fortunes of that house" (Ch. 49). His ability to accept limitations, to learn from suffering, marks Pip's gradual growth toward an integrated self. Pip learns to accept himself, not in terms of the false picturesque splendor of Satis House, but in its grotesque and actual condition. And he comes not to reject the marsh landscape of his birth, but to see his own limitations in terms of it. "My great expectations had all dissolved, like our own marsh mists before the sun" (Ch. 57).

When Pip loses his great expectations, he gains the possibility of becoming human. Under the influence of the illusion that he would have great wealth, he had acted in ways that led him away from himself:

> As I had grown accustomed to my expectations, I had insensibly begun to notice their effect upon myself and those around me. Their influence on my own character I disguised from my recognition as much as possible, but I knew very well that it was not all good.
>
> Ch. 34

To conceal from the world and from himself his own inadequacy in handling his new station, Pip plunges thoughtlessly into London life in the genial company of Herbert Pocket:

> We spent as much money as we could, and got as little for it as people could make up their minds to give us. We were always more or less miserable, and most of our acquaintance were in the same condition. There was a gay fiction among us that we were constantly enjoying ourselves, and a skeleton truth that we never did. To the best of my belief, our case was in the last respect a rather common one.
>
> Ch. 34

Acknowledging the world for what it is rather than the fictions others call it requires great self-assurance and self-knowledge. Until he loses his expectations, Pip is caught up in the general tendency to embellish rather than express the truth. He comes to London not quite trusting his own perceptions, for doing so would mean questioning received wisdom:

> We Britons had at that time particularly settled, that it was treasonable to doubt our having and our being the best of everything: otherwise, while I was scared by the immensity of London, I think I might have had some faint doubts whether it was not rather ugly, crooked, narrow, and dirty.
>
> Ch. 20

Guided to his rooms at Barnard's Inn, Pip is appalled by the dismal, dilapidated condition of the place:

> So imperfect was this realization of the first of my great expectations, that I looked in dismay at Mr. Wemmick. "Ah!" said he, mistaking me; "the retirement reminds you of the country. So it does me."
>
> Ch. 21

Wemmick's unconscious irony comically underscores the disparity between thing perceived and thing spoken. So often in this novel, as in the case of Barnard's Inn, that disparity results in the grotesque.

Pip's path to maturity, to realizing the world in all its imperfections, is not facilitated by people like Wemmick who woodenly adopt an inflexible stance toward the world. It is in that very rigidity, that fixed adherence to one idea that many of the characters make themselves grotesque. Wemmick's tag line, "Get hold of portable property," alerts us to the possibility of grotesquerie, for the world is too multifarious to make a single admonition generally useful. But it is in the sharp division between professional and private life that Wemmick's true grotesquerie arises. Both in Wemmick and in Jaggers, his employer, Dickens shows us prophetically modern types: people who say "the office is one thing, and private life is another" (Ch. 25). Lacking integration between the major parts of one's life, such a character is bound to be, as Wemmick is, grotesque. Comic, even wryly charming, but grotesque for all that.[29]

The "Castle" in which Wemmick lives carries some of the ideas of the Gothic Revival to absurd heights and interprets literally the notion that every man's home is his castle:

> Wemmick's house was a little wooden cottage in the midst of plots of garden, and the top of it was cut out and painted like a battery mounted with guns.... I think it was the smallest house I ever saw; with the queerest gothic windows (by far the greater part of them sham), and a gothic door, almost too small to get in at.
>
> Ch. 25

Wemmick's pride in creating this ingeniously devised dwelling is surpassed only by that of his father, whose notion on its preservation is better suited, as are the landscaping and the engineering of the Castle, to a noble estate. "This is a pretty pleasure-ground, sir. This spot and these beautiful works upon it ought to be kept together by the Nation, after my son's time, for the people's enjoyment'" (Ch. 25).

The comedy arises here, as it does in the instance of the Plornish Happy Cottage in *Little Dorrit,* from the disparity between the smallness of the dwelling and the largeness of the claims made for it. But while Happy Cottage represented the lower limits to which the picturesque sensibility extended, the Castle represents the total disjunction between private and professional life.

When Jaggers accidentally learns about his employee's private life, he professes astonishment:

> "*You* with a pleasant home?" said Mr. Jaggers.
>
> "Since it don't interfere with business," returned Wemmick, "let it be so. Now I look at you, sir, I shouldn't wonder if *you* might be planning and contriving to have a pleasant home of your own, one of these days, when you're tired of all this work."
>
> Ch. 51

Neither man can quite cope with the revelation of another sort of life outside the office, and Pip observes "that each of them seemed suspicious, not to say conscious, of having shown himself in a weak and unprofessional light to the other." At the end of the exchange, a client pleads, "A man can't help his feelings," and Jaggers lashes out, "I'll have no feelings here."

Jaggers' refusal to admit feelings, however admirable a lawyer it may make him, contributes also to making him a grotesque. His tag, the rule by which he lives, and the best advice he can offer Pip is to "Take nothing on its looks; take everything on evidence. There's no better rule" (Ch. 40). Years in the law have made Jaggers suspicious, cunning, and inclined to expect the worst of his fellows, but Pip feels uneasy in his presence, and ultimately rejects the coldly logical approach to life Jaggers offers him.[30]

The distorted focus on a single passion is bound up with a desire to impose one's will on other people. Both Jaggers and Miss Havisham, characters quite opposite in certain respects, share this impulse to dominate. Jaggers operates coolly, "rationally," in his thoroughgoing professional life, while Miss Havisham plays a highly emotional game from her narrow personal domain. Both understand the power of appearances, and manipulate them to affect their targets. Miss Havisham dresses up Estella in splendid jewels in order to attract Pip and break his heart, thus fulfilling her grotesquely single-minded vow of vengeance on all men. Jaggers stacks his case by dressing up witnesses to elicit certain reactions from the jury. Wemmick explains to Pip how Jaggers obtained an acquittal for Estella's mother:

> "It happened—happened, don't you see?—that this woman was so very artfully dressed from the time of her apprehension, that she looked much slighter than she really was; in particular, her sleeves are always remembered to have been so skilfully contrived that her arms had quite a delicate look."
>
> Ch. 48

Jaggers, the man who urges Pip to "take everything on evidence," creates the evidence he needs to win his cases. He knows most people are swayed by appearances, and he, like members of his profession before and since, plays to the stereotypical response expected from certain appearances.

This very manipulation of evidence through dress is what doomed Magwitch and preserved the wicked Compeyson. Their external appearance belies what they are. Though seeming handsome, Compeyson "[had] no more heart than a iron file, he was as cold as death, and he had the head of the Devil,'" according to Magwitch (Ch. 42). In short, possessing mechanical and deathly attributes rather than human ones, Compeyson is a grotesque. But it would take more than a casual observer to detect the flaw. Magwitch reports how the case was stacked against him:

> "When he was put in the dock, I noticed first of all what a gentleman Compeyson looked, wi' his curly hair and his black clothes and his white pocket-handkercher, and what a common sort of a wretch I looked. When the prosecution opened and the evidence was put short, aforehand, I noticed how heavy it all bore on me, and how light on him.
>
> Ch. 42

The jury, "taking everything on evidence," acquits Compeyson and condemns Magwitch. Pip, however, learns to judge by more subtle, more complex, more feeling means that lead him finally to distinguish substance from surface. To make this necessary, yet so often ignored, distinction, Pip must in effect experience another inversion of the world.

On a stormy night Pip is interrupted by an unexpected visitor at the foot of his stairs. Holding his lamp for the guest to ascend, Pip ushers into his gentleman's rooms the creature whose fixed idea it has been to make a gentleman:

> "Yes, Pip, dear boy, I've made a gentleman on you! It's me wot has done it! I swore that time, sure as ever I earned a guinea, that guinea should go to you.... I lived rough, that you should live smooth; I worked hard that you should be above work."
>
> Ch. 39

And suddenly Pip sees himself as a grotesque, a monster even, the creation of a convict's gold, and the ungrateful rejector of the faithful Joe. At that time his emotions are so disordered, his whole life turned so awry that the Frankenstein image in his mind stands uncertainly now for himself, now for Magwitch. "The imaginary student pursued by the misshapen creature he had impiously made, was not more wretched than I, pursued by the creature who had made me" (Ch. 40).

Yet this ultimate inversion that at a knock destroys all Pip's expectations, also announces the emergence from illusion that enables him to realize his essential humanity. Far from holding himself above the grotesque Magwitch, Pip comes to feel with him, almost losing his life for him. The change is shown in a remarkable picture that inverts the scene of Magwitch's arrival:

> We left him on the landing outside his door, holding a light over the stair-rail to light us down stairs. Looking back at him, I thought of the first night of his return, when our positions were reversed, and when I little supposed my heart could ever be as heavy and anxious at parting from him as it was now.
>
> Ch. 46

The scene is the exact reverse of that scene when Pip receives Magwitch and knows, to his utter despair, the author of his expectations.

Pip's initiation into the world does not stop with the lesson that seeming and being may differ. They may also be the same. Nowhere is evil more physically apparent than in Orlick—and here what you see is what he is. William Axton has made the provocative suggestion that Orlick represents in the destructive force of his thwarted expectations what Pip might have become.[31] "Thus at the limekiln Orlick becomes a kind of grotesquely exaggerated counterpart of Pip, or at least of that aspect of Pip's character which exhibits the 'bad side of human nature'—injustice—generally."

Orlick and Compeyson, self-made grotesques, remain faithful to their self-distortion to the end, the one showing it physically, the other not. Yet most grotesques in *Great Expectations* demonstrate the capacity to learn and, if not to change, at least to acknowledge what they have done. Pip's sister seems to repent for her abuse of him as she dies; Miss Havisham begs Pip's forgiveness in their last meeting; Magwitch, whose grotesquerie seems as much thrust upon him by a heartless society as by his own genetic inheritance, tries hard to leave something good behind him.

All of these characters affect Pip's own perception of himself and the part he is to play in the world. He threads his way past people who have willfully subverted their humanity to pursue a fixed idea. He suspects that even he, once a young man of great expectations, has, through his imperception and suffering, become a grotesque; and the awareness helps him reassert his common humanity. Instead of seeing himself as a being quite distinct from the criminal classes, he now feels closeness, even affection for Magwitch:

> For now my repugnance to him had all melted away, and in the hunted, wounded, shackled creature who held my hand in his, I only saw a man who had meant to be my benefactor, and who had felt affectionately, gratefully, and generously, towards me with great constancy through a series of years. I only saw in him a much better man than I had been to Joe.
>
> Ch. 54

Coming to recognize their shared humanity, Pip also comes to admire Magwitch for accepting the responsibility of his own life. Pip sees that "he pondered over the question whether he might have been a better man under better circumstances. But, he never justified himself by a hint tending that way, or tried to bend the past out of its eternal shape" (Ch. 56).

That lesson, too, Pip learns by the end. Instead of continuing to reject his earlier life at the forge, he arrives at the capacity to integrate his past with his present. On the river, where Herbert and Pip try to row Magwitch to freedom, Pip senses a link with his past:

> It was like my own marsh country, flat and monotonous, and with a dim horizon; while the winding river turned and turned, and the great floating buoys upon it turned and turned, and everything else seemed stranded and still. For, now, the last of the fleet of ships was round the last low point we had headed: and the last green barge, straw-laden, with a brown sail, had followed; and some ballast-lighters, shaped like a child's first rude imitation of a boat, lay low in the mud; and a little squat shoal-lighthouse on open piles, stood crippled in the mud on stilts and crutches; and slimy

> stakes stuck out of the mud, and red land-marks and tidemarks stuck out of the mud, and an old landing-stage and an old roofless building slipped into the mud, and all about us was stagnation and mud.
>
> We pushed off again, and made what way we could.
>
> Ch. 54

It is the topography of Pip's life—and, most likely, of our own lives. Not the wild, open seas of boundless possibility, but a world of "stagnation and mud" in which one makes what way one can. Such a setting was the fit repository for the body of a Quilp; here it shapes the soul of a Pip. The difference lies, as Pip learns, in what we make of such a world. We have one kind of life if we consider the "meshes" confining, imprisoning. We have quite another if we see instead the possibility of meshing with the rest of humanity. But this meshing is difficult for the quick and the sensitive. Although he accepts his commonness, his grotesqueness, although he desires to mesh with humanity, Pip does not return to the marshes to live, for he cannot. Life beckons beyond, and he becomes essentially a wanderer. Although the book has two endings, it really has no ending at all. Pip, like most of us, wanders the world without roots and tries to assert his humanity the best he can.

He learns to give love without expecting anything in return, to give as Joe, Biddy, and Herbert have given to him. Full humanity, so difficult to achieve, means giving more than expecting. It means learning to live with the rhythms of other people, not stolidly imposing one's rigid self upon them, not insisting on living by a single imperative: take everything on evidence; get hold of portable property; "love" with a consuming, ultimately self-devouring flame. Pursuing the single passion may produce colorful characters, but not people who wear well in society. Pip's recognition of this is a melancholy one. Bringing his own emotional expectations into balance makes him more mature and sober, but also more subdued. His emotional being is gentled—and also greyed. But perhaps that is the price of accepting full humanity rather than living under the propulsion of a single passion's illusory illumination.

Chapter Five
The Closing of the Circle: The Mystery of Edwin Drood

ETHELINDA,
Reverential Wife of
MR. THOMAS SAPSEA,
AUCTIONEER, VALUER, ESTATE AGENT, &c.,
of this city.
Whose Knowledge of the World,
Though somewhat extensive,
Never brought him acquainted with
A SPIRIT
More capable of
looking up to him.
STRANGER, PAUSE
And ask thyself the Question,
CANST THOU DO LIKEWISE?
If Not,
WITH A BLUSH RETIRE.

MR. SAPSEA'S epitaph for his wife might be taken as Dickens' own. But whether or not Dickens designed his own humorous epitaph, certain it is that his final novel bids farewell to the world. Datchery's extraordinary gesture of striking a chalk mark across an esoteric scoreboard ends the fragment with a grand flourish—as if the author recognized that his days had run out their number.

For the setting Dickens returns to the place where he began, to Rochester, the scene of his happiest childhood memories, the place in which he had set part of his first novel, and the location of his final, long-desired home, Gadshill. In the center of this half-finished novel Dickens describes former residents of the town in terms of a circular image that recurs throughout the book:

> To such as these, it has happened in their dying hours afar off, that they have imagined their chamber-floor to be strewn with the autumnal leaves fallen from the elm-trees in the Close: so have the rustling sounds and fresh scents of their earliest impressions revived when the circle of their lives was very nearly traced, and the beginning and the end were drawing close together.
>
> Ch. XIV

Dickens' circle was closing, giving an elegiac sense to the fragment, but we close this study of Dickens with *The Mystery of Edwin Drood*, not just from the fitness of things, but because in this final book Dickens drew together many of the visual motifs he had used earlier. Here, in the picturesque old town he calls Cloisterham, are conjoined the Gothic, the grotesque, and, poignantly, the Dance of Death. The opening vignette, with its background castle and foreground boats evokes the picturesque; yet the darkness of the plate suggests other associations, i.e., the boat of Charon and the river Styx.

Even though the conjunction of imagery recalls the use of similar motifs in earlier novels, *The Mystery of Edwin Drood* does not merely repeat earlier patterns. Just as his creation of a mystery represents a departure from his earlier forms as well as a connection to certain techniques in earlier novels such as *Oliver Twist*, so his visual imagery suggests continuity with that of his preceding career as well as the novelty of elements based on Empire. In 1870 the effects of the growing Empire were widely felt, and Dickens plays this element against traditional English insularity to create a spring of tension within the novel. The titular center of the novel, Edwin Drood, is planning to go out to Egypt as an engineer, much to the envy of his cousin, John Jasper, whose only association with Empire is his addiction to opium. Neville and Helena Landless have arrived in England from the eastern edges of the Empire, and their foreignness triggers racial animosity among the untravelled burghers of Cloisterham. How different in scale these wanderings of the globe from the minor peregrinations of Dickens' first sojourner in Rochester, Mr. Pickwick!

Cloisterham itself is the center of this novel, its Gothic architecture playing a more prominent part than in any novel since *The Old Curiosity Shop.* But the Gothic functions in quite different ways in the late novel and takes on complex meanings quite beyond the scope of the early book. In *The Old Curiosity Shop* the Gothic is invoked for its appeal to the picturesque sensibility and for its nostalgic associations with the past. But *The Mystery of Edwin Drood* gently ridicules such superficial appreciation of England's medieval art. Mr. Datchery comes to Cloisterham posing as an avowed lover of its picturesque ruins and seeking a lodging which is "odd and out of the way; something venerable, architectural and inconvenient" (Ch. XVIII). Cloisterham's Gothic architecture functions with a good deal more sophistication than the simplicity of these vaguely held objectives of the tourist would suggest. Indeed, the old town has the richness of landscape, and its residents reflect multiple facets of its time-honored existence. But Cloisterham is not a museum of the past appreciated only for its quaintness; it is a vital town valued as a continuum with the past, a stable point in a shifting world. And yet even this ancient town is feeling the effects of the future. Centrifugal forces are drawing away some residents and deeply affecting those who choose to remain. An implicit tension between settling in to venerable local traditions or sallying forth to enjoy the fruits of Empire charges these pages.

Although the Cloisterham cathedral itself attracts few to its services, it does serve as a fixed point by which to orient oneself in the physical world. Characters repeatedly locate themselves by reference to the cathedral. When they die, Cloisterham citizens can anticipate being laid to rest around the cathedral, thus achieving a continuity with the past and with the future which few outside cathedral towns can imagine. Cloisterham seems timeless and impervious to change; and yet, as Dickens says early in the novel, "A drowsy city, Cloisterham, whose inhabitants seem to suppose, with an inconsistency more strange than rare, that all its changes lie behind it, and that there are no more to come. A queer moral to derive from antiquity, yet older than any traceable antiquity" (Ch. III). "A city of another and a bygone time," yet being drawn into the present whether it will or not.

The opening chapter in which the cathedral appears in an opium dream prefigures the form of much that is to follow:

> An ancient English Cathedral Tower? How can the ancient English Cathedral tower be here! The well-known massive grey square tower of its old Cathedral? How can that be here! There is no spike of rusty iron in the air, between the eye and it, from any point of the real prospect. What is the spike that intervenes, and who has set it up? Maybe it is set up by the Sultan's orders for the impaling of a horde of Turkish robbers, one by one. It is so, for cymbals clash, and the Sultan goes by to his palace in long procession. Ten thousand scimitars flash in the sunlight, and thrice ten thousand dancing-girls strew flowers. Then, follow white elephants caparisoned in countless gorgeous colours, and infinite in number and attendants. Still the Cathedral Tower rises in the background, where it cannot be, and still no writhing figure is on the grim spike.

These most unEnglish images mingling with the Gothic Cathedral may come from Dickens' beloved Ali Baba. But they also suggest exotica from the Empire, a suggestion enhanced by the presence of a Chinaman and a Lascar in the opium den with John Jasper.

The picturesque aesthetic embraced the widely divergent styles of the Empire, giving us Chinese pagodas in Kew gardens and a mixture of Indian, Arabian, and Egyptian styles in Brighton Pavilion. Yet while such structures were designed to delight by their use of variety and surprise, this picturesque eclecticism engendered by Empire could create an array of such disorder as to move easily toward the grotesque. If the convergence of styles is so incongruous as to make the viewer begin to doubt his own visual perspective, the grotesque has become ascendant. This is what Dickens suggests with the opening description of violently distorted imagery.

Suitably situated in the midst of this grotesque confusion is John Jasper. Although he is employed as choirmaster in the cathedral, he finds that life too constraining and he therefore has recourse to another world opened to him through opium. His two worlds are reflected in the images of his dream, the "Gothic" part of which moves decidedly toward the grotesque—and the masochistic. Jasper sees a grim spike rising from the Cathedral Tower and wonders at there being no writhing figure on it. Even in its half-completed form, this novel shows us enough of Jasper to recognize his self-destructive tendencies. The grotesque, spiky features of Gothic architecture attract him as images of his own distorted soul. To Edwin he describes the monotony of his life, and the despair that accompanies it:

> "The echoes of my own voice among the arches seem to mock me with my daily drudging round. No wretched monk who droned his life away in that gloomy place, before me, can have been more tired of it than I am. He could take for relief (and did take) to carving demons out of the stalls and seats and desks. What shall I do? Must I take to carving them out of my heart?"
>
> Ch. II

Jasper's identification with Gothic grotesquerie is not to be taken lightly. In the course of the novel fragment he is described as a beast, a devil, and death. Those features of the Gothic which attract him, in addition to the grotesquerie, are the shadowy, the mysterious, the solemn:

> The old stone gatehouse in which he lives shadows the pendent masses of ivy and creeper covering the building's front. As the deep Cathedral-bell strikes the hour, a ripple of wind goes through these at their distance, like a ripple of the solemn sound that hums through tomb and tower, broken niche and defaced statue, in the pile close at hand.

Looking up at this dwelling, the Verger remarks, " 'There's his own solitary shadow betwixt his two windows—the one looking this way, and the one looking down into the High street—drawing his own curtains now' " (Ch. II). Even in its brevity this remarkable description suggests the duality of Jasper's nature, indication of which we have already glimpsed in the first chapter's presentation of him as a smoker of opium and a singer of hymns. We quickly are drawn inside the gatehouse where we see that "His room is a little sombre, and may have had its influence in forming his manner. It is mostly in shadow."

Jasper, in his own person and in the gloomy surroundings which reflect his character, resembles the villains of Gothic fiction. Darkly handsome and debonair, he conveys a slightly sinister air—but not to all. Rosa Bud senses it, though Edwin Drood does not. Jasper is not physically marked by his grotesquerie, as are Quilp, Bounderby, and Magwitch. This last of Dickens' villains carries still further the idea we noted in *Little Dorrit* and in *Great Expectations* that the handsome surface may conceal a heart full of guile.

The most marked contrast to Jasper is a man also in the employ of the church and also living in a Gothic structure. The Minor Canon, Mr. Crisparkle, lives contentedly with his mother in a dwelling reflective of their own amiability, one of those comfortable havens mellowed by time often glimpsed in a Dickens novel as a passing suggestion that domestic tranquillity is possible:

> Red-brick walls harmoniously toned down in colour by time, strong-rooted ivy, latticed windows, panelled rooms, big oaken beams in little places, and stone-walled gardens where annual fruit yet ripened upon monkish trees, were the principal surroundings of pretty old Mrs. Crisparkle and the Reverend Septimus.
>
> Ch. VI

Gothic architecture does not stifle the spirits of these two sturdy souls. But their island of timeless peace is invaded. Even though they live in quiet withdrawal, the Crisparkles are also caught up in change brought by the arrival of Neville Landless and their subsequent involvement in the disappearance of Edwin Drood.

Helena and Neville Landless arrive in Cloisterham from the Empire with the vague appearance of being "beautiful barbaric captives brought from some wild tropical dominion" (Ch. VI). Raised in Ceylon, they both present an exotic appearance in the cathedral town where frequent reference is made to their dark, quite unEnglish skin. Neither of them is really fit for the old town. Helena is sent to Miss Twinkleton's school, the Nuns' House, and her presence there only emphasizes the diminishing suitability of that establishment for the current age.

Even the delicate, dependent Rosa Bud, cast as the traditional little heroine of Gothic fiction, seems ill-prepared for entering the contemporary world by this anachronistic school. Most of the scenes set here are, tellingly, of people leaving. We never see a student at work;

indeed it is hard to imagine anything that the elegant, sophisticated Helena might find to do inside those walls. The Nuns' House is constructed of "venerable brick;" it has low ceilings and is filled with "odd angles and jutting gables" (Ch. III). And its gargoyles gentled by time contrast agreeably with Rosa Bud. "It would have made a pretty picture, so many pretty girls kissing Rosa in the cold porch of the Nuns' House, and that sunny little creature peeping out of it (unconscious of sly faces carved on spout and gable peeping at her)" (Ch. XIII).

The Nuns' House, for all its conventual associations, cannot protect Rosa from her most dreaded pursuer, John Jasper, and the old Gothic pile serves as backdrop for a most extraordinary meeting in the garden. Leading up to this meeting is a description of the summer day which introduces the figure of an as yet benignant reaper:

> Time was when travel-stained pilgrims rode in clattering parties through the city's welcome shades; time is when wayfarers, leading a gipsy life between haymaking time and harvest, and looking as if they were just made of the dust of the earth, so very dusty are they, lounge about on cool door-steps, trying to mend their unmendable shoes, or giving them to the city kennels as a hopeless job, and seeking others in the bundles that they carry, along with their yet unused sickles swathed in bands of straw.
>
> Ch. XIX

The passage occurs at the beginning of a chapter entitled "Shadow on the Sun-dial," and these references to Time and sickles are carefully chosen to work in conjunction with the shadowy Jasper whose pose on the sun-dial is as Death's traditional pose with the hourglass. When Rosa first sees him "leaning on the sun-dial, the old horrible feeling of being compelled by him, asserts its hold upon her." Dressed in deep mourning, he looks the figure of death, or the devil—"...his face looks so wicked and menacing, as he stands leaning against the sun-dial—setting, as it were, his black mark upon the very face of day—that her flight is arrested by horror as she looks at him."

This scene in which Jasper terrifies Rosa into a faint, quite literally taking her breath away, adds to the steady accretion of images associating Jasper with the traditional figure of Death. It is an association that places him in the company of such characters as Henry Gowan and Mr. Vholes who were content, unlike Jasper, with killing the spirit. Jasper's participation in an adapted version of the Dance of Death seems a natural extension from the medieval Gothic and grotesque surroundings which characterize him. He is "conducted" through the "Dance" by a stone-mason nicknamed "Stony" Durdles whose eccentricities and whose dependence on death for his living make us suspect that Dickens intended him as a surrogate for Death, a suspicion heightened by Durdles' odd uncertainty about himself. "He often speaks of himself in the third person; perhaps, being a little misty as to his own identity when he narrates, perhaps impartially adopting the Cloisterham nomenclature in reference to a character of acknowledged distinction" (Ch. IV). Durdles' "distinction" arises from his occupation, which makes him the best-known creature in Cloisterham.[1] "Durdles is a stonemason; chiefly in the gravestone, tomb, and monument way, and wholly of their colour from head to foot. No man is better known in Cloisterham. He is the chartered libertine of the place. Fame trumpets him a wonderful workman" (Ch. IV). Like Death, who traditionally is designated a "libertine," and who also has free rein, the stony-colored Durdles has an uncanny knowledge of and familiarity with the dead buried in the walls of Cloisterham. He takes peculiar pride in showing Jasper the stones he has carved, much as if he were listing the participants of an already enacted Dance of Death:

> "Durdles was making his reflections here when you come up, sir, surrounded by his words, like a poplar Author.—Your own brother-in-law...Mrs. Sapsea...Late Incumbent;" introducing the Reverend Gentleman's broken column. "Departed Assessed Taxes;" introducing a vase and towel..."Former pastrycook and Muffin-maker...all safe and sound here, sir, and all Durdles's work."
>
> Ch. IV

Various people from various walks of life are enumerated as if Durdles had, "like a poplar author," decreed the time and created the setting of their demise. Yet Durdles has the impartial, detached attitude of Death that comes, indifferently, to all alike; whereas Jasper seems bent on directed malevolence. They might as a pair best be represented as Death and the Devil.

The dwelling of Durdles is at one point explicitly connected with the Dance of Death, and another time described as containing personified figures in the yard. "Herein two journeymen incessantly chip, while two other journeymen, who face each other, incessantly saw stones, dipping as regularly in and out of their sheltering sentry-boxes as if they were mechanical figures emblematical of Time and Death" (Ch. IV). Later references to these journeymen stone-cutters tie them more closely to Holbein, particularly to his small drawings done for "The Alphabet of Death."

Holbein's side border shows Death accosting a victim under a Gothic arch so small as to give the sense of a sentry-box. Death in the lower right-hand corner carries a pickax, the very instrument often carried about by Durdles.

> Thus he will say, touching his strange sights: "Durdles came upon the old chap," in reference to a buried magnate of ancient time and high degree, "by striking right into the coffin with his pick. The old chap gave Durdles a look with his open eyes, as much as to say, 'Is your name Durdles? Why, my man, I've been waiting for you a devil of a time!' And then he turned to powder."
>
> Ch. IV

Durdles has some of the attributes of Holbein's Death, but he unwittingly passes on some of his knowledge to one who would assume the prerogatives of Death, John Jasper:

> Repairing to Durdles's unfinished house, or hole in the city wall, and seeing a light within it, he [Jasper] softly picks his course among the grave-stones, monuments, and stony lumber of the yard, already touched here and there, sidewise, by the rising moon. The two journeymen have left their two great saws sticking in their blocks of stone; and two skeleton journeymen out of the Dance of Death might be grinning in the shadow of their sheltering sentry-boxes, about to slash away at cutting out the gravestones of the next two people destined to die in Cloisterham. Likely enough, the two think little of that now, being alive, and perhaps merry.
>
> Ch. XII

The allusion to the unwitting victims in Durdles' yard with its emblems of the Dance of Death is not happenstance; for Jasper, the potential murderer, is at that moment arriving for an expedition with Durdles, who appears on this occasion "Like a Ghoule."

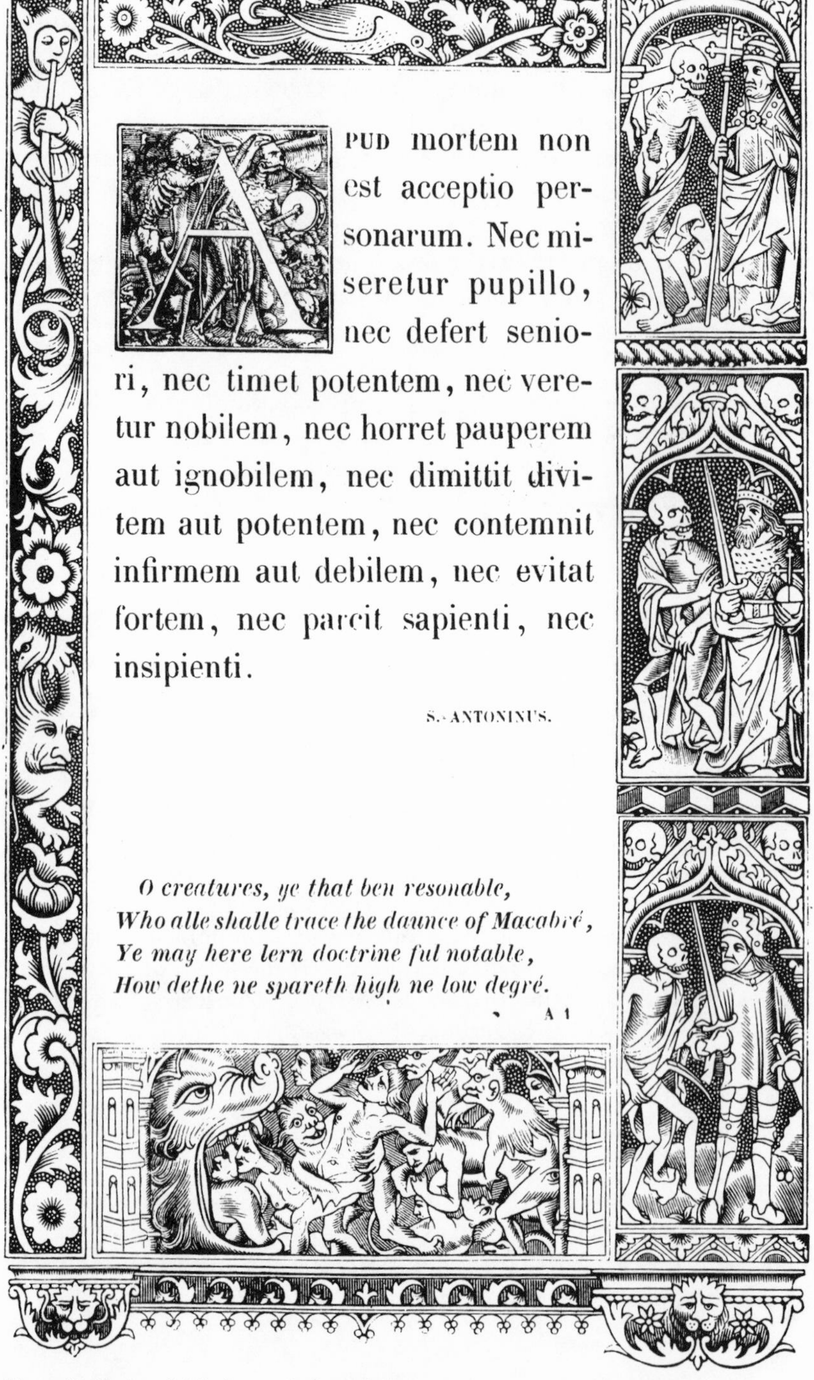

APUD mortem non est acceptio personarum. Nec miseretur pupillo, nec defert seniori, nec timet potentem, nec veretur nobilem, nec horret pauperem aut ignobilem, nec dimittit divitem aut potentem, nec contemnit infirmem aut debilem, nec evitat fortem, nec parcit sapienti, nec insipienti.

S. ANTONINUS.

O creatures, ye that ben resonable,
Who alle shalle trace the daunce of Macabré,
Ye may here lern doctrine ful notable,
How dethe ne spareth high ne low degré.

A 1

Hans Holbein, "A" from "The Alphabet of Death," The Beinecke Rare Book and Manuscript Library, Yale University

The expressed reason for this expedition is Jasper's love of the picturesque, and his desire to see such effects under the tutelage of Durdles. In fact, the probable purpose of this "unaccountable sort of expedition" is Jasper's desire to find a suitable burial place for his intended victim. Like Datchery, then, Jasper fakes his interest in the picturesque to conceal other, unnamed purposes, a piece of deception suitable to 1870 when the cult of the picturesque was waning. The moonlight expedition, though taken under picturesque auspices, is in reality a kind of Dance of Death. That it is the handsome Jasper, rather than the wraith-like Durdles who is cast as Death in this sequence is seen in the peculiar behavior and expression of Jasper shortly after he meets up with Durdles. They see approaching, and conceal themselves from, Mr. Crisparkle, the Minor Canon, and the despised Neville:

> Jasper folds his arms upon the top of the wall, and, with his chin resting on them, watches. He takes no note whatever of the Minor Canon, but watches Neville, as though his eye were at the trigger of a loaded rifle, and he had covered him, and were going to fire. A sense of destructive power is so expressed in his face, that even Durdles pauses in his munching, and looks at him.
>
> Ch. XII

Like Holbein's personification of Death, Jasper singles out a particular victim, ignoring the companion, and as the pair continue on their way "bursts into a fit of laughter," the sort Dickens labeled in *Nicholas Nickleby* "ominous mirth."

Jasper and Durdles move on into the medieval Cathedral where the shadows cast by the moonlight create a striking picture in black and white with the quality of a Holbein woodcut.

> They enter, locking themselves in, descend the rugged steps, and are down in the Crypt. The lantern is not wanted, for the moonlight strides in at the groined windows, bare of glass, the broken frames for which cast patterns on the ground. The heavy pillars which support the roof engender masses of black shade, but between them there are lanes of light.
>
> Ch. XII

Pacing these Gothic lanes, Durdles discoursing on the dead he means to disinter, Jasper covertly searching for a suitable place of interment, the pair seem to be recreating a scene from the Dance of Death. This suggestion is further enhanced when they emerge on the Cathedral level:

> Here, the moonlight is so very bright again that the colours of the nearest stained-glass window are thrown upon their faces. The appearance of the unconscious Durdles, holding the door open for his companion to follow, as if from the grave, is ghastly enough, with a purple band across his face, and a yellow splash upon his brow.
>
> Ch. XII

Once again, it is difficult to say which of this macabre pair is playing out the role of Death, or, again, whether they represent Death and the Devil. The latter suggestion is reinforced when they at last emerge from this strange expedition and see "a hideous small boy... dancing in the moonlight." Jasper calls this stone-throwing boy "a baby-devil" and becomes so angry "that he seems an older devil himself" (Ch. XII).

In the closing pages of this novel fragment there occurs an image with the slightest suggestion of the Dance of Death, an image easily overlooked, yet one which seems suggestive taken in context with the above passages. The devilish stone-throwing boy is seen outside the cathedral, announcing to a detective the presence of an old woman, whom we know to have come from Jasper's opium den in order to spy on him and betray him. Having announced her arrival the boy "breaks into a slow and stately dance, perhaps supposed to be performed by the Dean" (Ch. XXIII). Given the context, the boy's motions suggest a Death Dance and imply that this time Jasper may be the unwitting victim, that instead of his continuing to play Death, or the Devil, he is now to be claimed by Death. But the novel fragment ends here, and we are never to know.

In putting such heavy stress on the Dance of Death in conjunction with an old Gothic town—and particularly with an old Gothic church, Dickens was projecting graphically his despair with the institutional church. He still retained the belief that certain individual clergymen such as the Minor Canon were men of probity and dignity, but even they were curiously ineffectual. They lived on like relics from another age, as mellowed by time as their dwelling places—and as incongruous in the changing age. If there can be Mr. Crisparkles, there can also be John Jaspers, whose intimate association with the church only heightens his self-hatred. Crisparkle may possess that genial acceptance of mediocrity endemic among the clergy, but Jasper is ambitious and feels constrained by the cloistered atmosphere of the town where he must dwell. The grotesquerie associated with the Gothic therefore gives him his clearest image of himself: not acceptant of creedal Christianity endorsed by time, but tortuously insistent on asserting his own distorted, ugly variance from belief.

The Gothic ruins in *The Old Curiosity Shop* were neither functional nor inspiriting, but at least they offered a refuge for the weary. In *The Mystery of Edwin Drood* little salutary effect is discernible. Gothic architecture comes to us first inextricably joined with the grotesque in a bizarre image spinning out of an opium dream. At the end of the first chapter the Gothic cathedral serves as the setting for a liturgy the emphasis of which is on human evil rather than redemption. Death and wickedness are the themes appropriated by this church; life and goodness exist outside it.

Dickens had expressed his profound disenchantment with the church in a letter written to W.F. Cerjat just a few years before he wrote his last novel:

> As to the Church, my friend, I am sick of it....that the Church's hand is at its own throat I am fully convinced. Here, more Popery, there, more Methodism—as many forms of consignment to eternal damnation as there are articles, and all in one forever quarreling body—the Master of the New Testament put out of sight...these things cannot last. The Church that is to have its part in the coming time must be a more Christian one, with less arbitrary pretentions and a stronger hold upon the mantle of our Saviour, as he walked and talked upon this earth.[2]

What he expressed to Cerjat, Dickens visualized in *The Mystery of Edwin Drood.* By means of the Gothic, the grotesque, and the Dance of Death Dickens criticized the contemporary church, contrasting it with the freshness and beauty of the surrounding landscape:

> In the free outer air, the river, the green pastures, and the brown arable lands, the teeming hills and dales, were reddened by the sunset: while the distant little windows in windmills and farm homesteads, shone, patches of bright beaten gold. In the Cathedral, all

> became grey, murky, and sepulchral, and the cracked monotonous mutter went on like a dying voice, until the organ and the choir burst forth, and drowned it in a sea of music.[3]
>
> Ch. IX

In his appreciation of natural beauty Dickens was not adopting a pagan view; rather, he saw in nature evidence of the eternal Resurrection, poignant evidence of which occurs on the next to last page he ever wrote:

> A brilliant morning shines on the old city. Its antiquities and ruins are surpassingly beautiful, with a lusty ivy gleaming in the sun, and the rich trees waving in the balmy air. Changes of glorious light from moving boughs, songs of birds, scents from gardens, woods, and fields—or, rather, from the one great garden of the whole cultivated island in its yielding time—penetrate into the Cathedral, subdue its earthy odour, and preach the Resurrection and the Life. The cold stone tombs of centuries ago grow warm; and flecks of brightness dart into the sternest marble corners of the building, fluttering there like wings.
>
> Ch. XXIII

"The whole cultivated island" embraces the conjoined efforts of man and nature, town and country, appreciating the special beauty England possesses through its "antiquities and ruins." This passage celebrates the pleasing combination of natural movement and mellowing age that were valued by the picturesque before it became corrupted.

But the resolution does not rest here. On Dickens' final page we get a return to grotesquerie with a description of the opium woman shaking her fist at Jasper from behind a grotesque carving. Dickens' final pages thus circle back to a conjunction of the imagery used in his first novel: a positive picturesque landscape redolent of hope and ongoing life juxtaposed with a grotesque. Dickens, the painter of scenes celebrating the wonder of life, and Dickens, the moral reformer bent on shaking people out of their delusions by making them see, stand counterbalanced in his last images as they stood throughout his extraordinary career.

Notes

Introduction

1. A useful collection of papers demonstrating the interdisciplinary interest of the Victorian amateur is *The Mind and Art of Victorian England,* ed. Josef L. Altholz (Minneapolis: University of Minnesota Press, 1976).
2. "An Idea of Mine," *Household Words,* XVII (13 Mar. 1858), 416; rpt. *Collected Papers,* 2 vols. (Bloomsbury: Nonesuch Press, 1937), I, 699.
3. Dickens' view has been echoed by others, notably by Raymond Lister who sees the Victorian narrative picture as "a reassuring series of distorting mirrors held up by the Victorians to the world around them, glossing over what was nasty and frequently distorting real feeling into mushy sentimentality." *Victorian Narrative Paintings* (London: Museum Press Ltd., 1966), 9.
4. *The Letters of Charles Dickens,* ed. Walter Dexter, 3 vols. (Bloomsbury: Nonesuch Press, 1938), II, 700. Hereafter designated *Nonesuch Letters.* William Michael Rossetti made similar observations. See his notes pencilled in the margin of *Explication des Ouvrages de Peinture, Sculpture, Gravure, Lithographie et Architecture des Artists Vivants, Etrangers et Francais* (Paris, 1855) in Beinecke Library, New Haven.
5. E.H. Gombrich, *Meditations on a Hobby Horse* (London: Phaidon, 1963), 26.
6. (Berkeley: University of California Press, 1969), 13.
7. *Ibid.,* 134.
8. Cited both by T.S.R. Boase, *English Art 1800–1870* (Oxford: Clarendon Press, 1959), 288 note; and by Wendell Stacy Johnson, "The Bride of Literature: Ruskin, the Eastlakes, and mid-Victorian Theories of Art," *Victorian Newsletter* (Fall, 1964), 23.
9. *The Hero in Eclipse in Victorian Fiction,* trans. Angus Davidson (London: Oxford University Press, 1956), 29.

10. *The Speeches of Charles Dickens,* ed. K.J. Fielding (Oxford: Clarendon Press, 1960), 422.
11. 10 Jan. 1856, *Nonesuch Letters,* II, 727.
12. 15 April 1869, *Nonesuch Letters,* III, 719.
13. "Aspects of Analogy: The Changing Role of the Sister Arts Tradition in Victorian Criticism," *English Studies in Canada,* III (1978), 60.
14. See Jean Hagstrum, *The Sister Arts* (Chicago: University of Chicago Press, 1958).
15. See, for instance, "Becky in Her Second Appearance as Clytemnestra" in *Vanity Fair.*
16. *The Speeches of Charles Dickens,* 13.
17. *Ibid.,* 19.
18. *Ibid.,* 157.
19. The National Gallery opened in 1838, but John Steegman takes 1832, the year of the first Reform Bill, as marking a significant change. "It was the middle-class patronage that controlled henceforward for many years the Arts." *The Rule of Taste from George I to George IV* (London: Macmillan, 1936), 186.
20. *English Art 1800-1870,* 171.
21. (Architectural Press, 1956), rpt. (Harmondsworth: Penguin, 1964), 36.
22. *Ibid.,* 46.
23. *Ibid.,* 36.
24. David A. Roos, "Dickens at the Royal Academy of Arts; A New Speech and Two Eulogies," *The Dickensian,* 73 (May 1977), 107.
25. *Bleak House,* Ch. XII. Unless otherwise noted, all citations from Dickens' novels are from the Oxford Illustrated Edition (London: Oxford University Press, 1947-1957).
26. See the chapter entitled "Ruskin and the Picturesque" in Robert Hewison, *John Ruskin: the Argument of the Eye* (London: Thames and Hudson, 1976).
27. *Allegory, the Theory of a Symbolic Mode* (Ithaca: Cornell University Press, 1964), 23.
28. *The Grotesque in English Literature* (London: Oxford University Press, 1965), 221.

Chapter One

1. See Henry David Thoreau, *Cape Cod* (Boston: Houghton Miflin, 1893; copyright 1864), 141.
2. Frederick Law Olmsted, *Forty Years of Landscape Architecture: Central Park* (Cambridge: MIT Press, 1973; first published 1928), 46.

3. See John Dixon Hunt, *The Figure in the Landscape:* Poetry, Painting, and Gardening during the 18th Century (Baltimore: Johns Hopkins Press, 1976); and *The Genius of the Place: the English Landscape Garden, 1620–1820,* ed. John Dixon Hunt and Peter Willis (New York: Harper and Row, 1975).
4. See Elizabeth Manwaring, *Italian Landscape in 18th-Century England:* a Study of the Influence of Claude Lorrain and Salvator Rosa on English Taste, 1700–1800 (New York: Oxford, 1925); and Lynne Epstein, "Mrs. Radcliffe's Landscapes: The Influence of Three Landscape Painters on Her Nature Descriptions," *Hartford Studies in Literature,* I (1969), 106–120.
5. See his remarks in *Walden,* such as, "William Gilpin, who is so admirable in all that relates to landscape, and usually so correct..." *The Writings of Henry David Thoreau* (Boston: Houghton Miflin, 1893), Vol. 2, 317.
6. (London: printed for J. Robson, 1768), 2.
7. (London: printed for R. Blamir, 1792), 3.
8. *Ibid.,* 26.
9. Printed by Uvedale Price together with *A Dialogue on the Distinct Characters of the Picturesque and the Beautiful, in Answer to the Objections of Mr. Knight* (London, 1801), 89.
10. "...*picturesque beauty* [occurs] in visible objects, because painting, by imitating the visible qualities only, discriminates it from the objects of other senses with which it may be combined." *Ibid.,* 95.
11. Uvedale Price, *A Dialogue,* 131.
12. "The Picturesque Moment," *From Sensibility to Romanticism,* ed. Frederick W. Hilles and Harold Bloom (New York: Oxford University Press, 1965), 285.
13. *The Picturesque* (London: G.P. Putnam, 1927), 2.
14. See Sergei Eisenstein, "Dickens, Griffith and the Film Today," *Film Form and the Film Sense,* trans. and ed. Jay Leyda (New York: Meridian Books, 1957); William C. Wees, "Dickens, Griffith and Eisenstein: Form and Image in Literature and Film," *Humanities Association Bulletin,* 24 (1973), 266–276; Ana L. Zambrano, "Charles Dickens and Sergei Eisenstein: the Emergence of Cinema," *Style,* 9 (1974), 469–482.
15. See "Tintern Abbey" and "The Prelude," Book 12.
16. *Athenaeum,* 26 Mar. 1836.
17. John Steegman remarks that "As late as the 1870's, it was possible to publish a guide-book with such a title as *Black's Picturesque Tourist in England.*" *The Rule of Taste,* 113.
18. The observation is also made by Jane Rabb Cohen, "Dickens and his Original Illustrators," (Harvard: unpub. doctoral dissertation, 1968); and by Harold Child, "Caricature and the Literature of Sport: *Punch,*" *Cam-*

bridge History of English Literature, ed. A.W. Ward and A.R. Waller (Cambridge University Press, 1932), XIV, 218; and see also B.C. Saywood, "Dr. Syntax: A Pickwickian Prototype?" *Dickensian* 66 (Jan. 1970), 24–29.

19. Edgar Johnson, *Charles Dickens, His Tragedy and Triumph,* 2 vols. (New York: Simon and Schuster, 1952), I, 115–119.
20. Unhappily, this reversal of roles proved disastrous for the unstable Seymour. Already depressed by many other matters, Seymour was irrationally agitated by Dickens' insistence on the revision of a design. A few days after submitting a second plate for "The Dying Clown," Seymour took his own life.
21. The oval shape of the music cover design, and indeed of most illustrations to Dickens' fiction, probably owes something to the shape of the Claude glass.
22. W.H. Pyne listed 1000 possible elements in his Picturesque Groups for the Embellishment of Landscape. Cited by Hussey, 118.
23. Ruskin also perceived the moral danger inherent in the picturesque. Robert Hewison says, "Ruskin's first line of attack on the picturesque, then, was that it was a false vision of nature, the product of an approach which made only a superficial study of the outward forms of natural scenery, and then only to select certain aspects to compose into an idealized picture which bore no resemblance to the 'facts.'" *John Ruskin: the Argument of the Eye,* 46.
24. Speech delivered on behalf of the Hospital for Sick Children, 9 Feb. 1858. *The Speeches of Charles Dickens,* 250.
25. John Forster, *The Life of Charles Dickens,* ed. J.W.T. Ley (London: Cecil Palmer, 1928), 586.
26. "Genoa and Its Neighbourhood," *Pictures from Italy.*
27. 11 Feb. 1845, *The Life of Charles Dickens,* 370.
28. *Ibid.*
29. To Miss Coutts, 18 Mar. 1845, *Nonesuch Letters,* I, 665.
30. See, for instance, Ch. XII of *Bleak House* and "An Idea of Mine," *Household Words,* XVII (13 Mar. 1858), 416.
31. 27 April 1855, *Nonesuch Letters,* II, 655. My underlining.
32. *Charles Dickens, His Tragedy and Triumph,* II, 846.
33. John Holloway, in a note to the Penguin edition of *Little Dorrit,* 1967, says Fanny's phrase may be "a corruption of *Love in a Village,* a comedy by Isaac Bickerstaafe, 1763." More likely, Fanny's phrase is intended to evoke a picturesque impression, particularly as her emotional response to the image of Pet is the coolly detached, "interesting."
34. April 1856, *Nonesuch Letters,* II, 765.
35. Dickens wrote to Forster on his second Italian trip, "Your guide-book writer, representing the general swarming of humbugs...(bound to follow

Eustace, Forsyth, and all the rest of them) directs you, on pain of being broke for want of gentility in appreciation, to go into ecstacies with things that have neither imagination, nature, proportion, possibility, nor anything else in them. You immediately obey, and tell your son to obey. He tells his son, and he tells his, and so the world gets at three-fourths of its frauds and miseries." 28 Nov. 1853, *The Life of Charles Dickens,* 586–587. Dickens refers to John Chatwode Eustace, whose *Classical Tour through Italy,* issued in 1817 in four volumes, was widely used.

36. David Jarrett discusses this novel in terms of the Gothic conventions of Mrs. Radcliffe and concludes with an observation similar to the position taken in this book. "Dickens was able to adopt Gothic conventions not to undermine, but to intensify his portrayal of reality." "The Fall of the House of Clennam: Gothic Conventions in *Little Dorrit,*" *The Dickensian,* 73 (Sept. 1977), 161.

Chapter Two

1. *The Victorian Treasure House* (London: Collins, 1973), 105. See, especially Chapter 3, "The City and the Picturesque," 65–105.
2. *The Grotesque in Art and Literature,* trans. Ulrich Weisstein (Bloomington: University of Indiana Press, 1963), 11.
3. *Ibid.,* 122.
4. See *The Grotesque in English Literature.*
5. *The Grotesque in Art and Literature,* 37.
6. *Ibid.,* 181.
7. *The Grotesque in English Literature,* 65.
8. *Ibid.,* 73.
9. *Ibid.,* 17.
10. *Ibid.,* 70.
11. *The Complete Works,* 39 vols. ed. E.T. Cook and Alexander Wedderburn (London: George Allen, 1903–1912), V, 138. Hereafter designated *Works.*
12. *The Grotesque in Art and Literature,* 24.
13. Dickens first wrote this in a letter to Forster who later printed it in *The Life of Charles Dickens,* 490–491. The essay, "Cruikshank's 'The Drunkard's Children,'" appeared in *Household Words,* July 8, 1848, and has been reprinted in *Collected Papers* I, 157–160. The passage quoted here appears on 158–159.
14. Forster speaks of seeing them at Gadshill, and Hans Andersen at Tavistock House. Elias Bredsdorff, *Hans Andersen and Charles Dickens* (Copenhagen: Rosenkilde and Bagger, 1956), 89.
15. 16 July 1841, *The Letters of Charles Dickens,* Pilgrim edition, 4 vols. to

date, ed. Madeline House and Graham Storey (Oxford: Clarendon Press, 1965–), II, 361 note. Hereafter called *Pilgrim Letters.*

16. 31 Jan. 1841, *Pilgrim Letters,* II, 201.
17. *Pilgrim Letters,* I, 431.
18. "Charles Dickens," *A New Spirit of the Age* (London: Smith, Elder and Co., 1844), I, 7.
19. "Dickens' Tales," *Edinburgh Review,* LXVIII (Oct. 1838), 76.
20. *Hogarth and His Place in European Art* (London: Basic Books, 1962), 189.
21. "On the Genius and Character of Hogarth," *Anecdotes of William Hogarth,* ed. J.B. Nichols (London: J.B. Nichols, 1833), 104–105.
22. "On the Works of Hogarth: on the Grand and Familiar Style of Painting," *The Miscellaneous Works* (London: G. Routledge and Sons, 1887), 149.
23. "Exaggerated Character: A Study of the Works of Dickens and Hogarth," *Centennial Review,* 20 (1976), 293.
24. See Hogarth's "Characters and Caricaturas" (1743), and Fielding's preface to *Joseph Andrews* where he defends himself and Hogarth against the charge of caricature.
25. In the same vein, see Dickens' remarks in *Pilgrim Letters,* IV, 5.
26. "Unto This Last," 1860, *Works,* XVII, 31 note.
27. "Dickens' Tales," 76–77.
28. "Charles Dickens," *A New Spirit of the Age,* I, 11.
29. William Frith, for instance, complained in his autobiography about the restrictions placed on painters by the proprieties of the age:

    > I know very well that if I or any other painter dared to introduce certain incidents (such as bristle over Hogarth's works) into our pictures, they would have no chance of shocking the public that admires the Hogarths on the walls in Trafalgar Square, for the Council of the Royal Academy would prevent any such catastrophe.

    My Autobiography and Reminiscences, 3 vols. (London: R. Bentley, 1887), II, 17.
30. Or Cruikshank had suggested–the true inventor will probably never be known, though Richard Vogler has presented compelling evidence for seeing the illustrator as the progenitor of this controversial tale. See "*Oliver Twist:* Cruikshank's Pictorial Prototypes," *Dickens Studies Annual,* II (1972), 98–118.
31. *The Newgate Novel, 1830–1847* (Detroit: Wayne State University Press, 1963), 14.
32. *Ibid.,* 15.
33. See R.H. Horne, "Charles Dickens," 18; Antal, 251, note 52; Jane Rabb Cohen, 40.

34. Dickens, with Wilkie Collins, used this theme later in "The Lazy Tour of Two Idle Apprentices," *Household Words,* XVI (Oct. 1857), 393.
35. See Ronald Paulson's interpretation in *Hogarth: His Life, Art, and Times,* abridged ed. (New Haven: Yale, 1974), 254–255.
36. 1841 Preface to the third edition.
37. In spite of Dickens' insistence upon the reality of this environment, various critics have argued convincingly that the novel is best understood symbolically. John Bayley denies that Dickens is showing us "things as they really are," yet admits the power of his social protest. Bayley acknowledges the successful fusion of imagery and protest: "...the main feat—surely unique in the history of the novel—which Dickens has achieved in combining the genre of Gothic nightmare with that of social denunciation, so that each enhances the other." "*Oliver Twist:* 'Things as They Really Are'," in *Dickens: A Collection of Critical Essays*, ed. Martin Price (Englewood Cliffs: Prentice-Hall, 1967), 96.

    Arnold Kettle says, "What we get from *Oliver Twist* is not a greater precision of sensitiveness about the day-to-day problems of human behavior but a sharpened sense of the larger movement of life within which particular problems arise." "Dickens: *Oliver Twist,*" *An Introduction to the English Novel* (London, 1951), Vol. I, rpt. in *The Dickens Critics,* ed. George H. Ford and Lauriat Lane, Jr. (Ithaca: Cornell University Press, 1961), 255.

    J. Hillis Miller suggests an antagonism between popular melodrama and historical verisimilitude. Later he suggests that "The fundamental question in this novel is whether anyone can break the iron chain of metonymy whereby a person is inevitably like his envrionment," "The Fiction of Realism: *Sketches by Boz, Oliver Twist,* and Cruikshank's Illustrations," *Dickens Centennial Essays,* ed. Ada Nisbet and Blake Nevius (Berkeley: University of California Press, 1971), 115.
38. Denis Donoghue quotes from Mill and Wordsworth to show the necessity of cultivating the feelings in an Age of Science, and then goes on to say, "The continuity between *Lyrical Ballads* and Dickens' novels is based upon this conviction that the flow of feeling may still dissolve the frozen places of life." "The English Dickens and *Dombey and Son,*" *Dickens Centennial Essays,* 11.
39. F.R. Leavis has also noted that this novel contains many Hogarthian undertones, but his suggestive article does not explore the correspondence in depth or detail. See *"Dombey and Son," Sewanee Review,* 70 (1962), 177–201.
40. Originally Dickens intended for Walter to end as a wastrel, in which case his story would be highly similar to Hogarth's Idle 'Prentice. See his letter to Forster, 25 July 1846, *Nonesuch Letters,* I, 771. So, too, his plan for

Edith was originally much more Hogarthian. Dickens had intended to have Edith commit adultery and then die. See Harry Stone, "The Novel as Fairy-Tale: Dickens' *Dombey and Son,*" *English Studies,* XLVII (Feb. 1966), 9.

41. For suggestive links to graphic satire in this incident see Michael Steig, "*Dombey and Son* and the Railway Panic of 1845," *The Dickensian,* 67 (Sept. 1971), 145-148.
42. Michael Steig makes a provocative suggestion about the relationship of men and women in this novel. "The explicit theme of *Dombey and Son* seems to be that mercenary and power-hungry men like Dombey and Carker make victims of women." He goes on to suggest that the subtext of the illustrations implies "that such men are simultaneously the prey of these women." See *Dickens and Phiz* (Bloomington: Indiana University Press, 1978), 112.

Chapter Three

1. See Emile Mâle, *L'Art Religieux de la Fin du Moyen Age en France* (Paris: 1925), 361; Alfred Scott Warthin, *The Physician of the Dance of Death* (New York: Arno Press, 1977; first pub. 1931), 10.
2. *The Life of Charles Dickens,* 12.
3. *Pilgrim Letters,* I, 9.
4. *Ibid.,* II, note 229.
5. See James M. Clark, *The Dance of Death* (London: Phaidon, 1947), 23-32.
6. *The Physician of the Dance of Death,* 52.
7. *Ibid.,* 92.
8. Lauriat Lane has observed that this preface looks back on *The Pickwick Papers* and sees, "imaginatively and intuitively ordered there, Holbein's vision." See "Mr. Pickwick and the Dance of Death," *Nineteenth-Century Fiction,* 14 (Sept. 1959), 172.
9. Book II, Ch. XXIII.
10. See Henri Stegemeier, *The Dance of Death in Folksong* (University of Chicago dissertation, 1939), 188-206.
11. R.H. Horne described Scadder as "drawn with the tangible truth of Hans Holbein," "Charles Dickens," *A New Spirit of the Age,* I, 53.
12. Curiously, Holbein was considered by many English to be Dutch. The mistake came about in an interesting way. F. Douce remarks in his preface to the 1804 edition of *The Dance of Death* that Holbein

    painted a Dance of Death in fresco, upon the walls of the Palace at Whitehall, which was consumed by fire in 1697. This curious fact

> is ascertained from 2 sets of 19 very indifferent etchings from the wooden cuts, by one Nieuhoff; they were never published, but copies of them were presented to the artist's friends, with manuscript dedications in the Dutch language, in which he speaks of the above-mentioned paintings at Whitehall.

"Notes," *The Dance of Death* (London: John Harding, 1804), 24–25. This association of the Dutch language with Holbein's *Dance of Death* must have contributed to the notion that Holbein was himself Dutch.

Earlier than the Nieuhoff episode there had been another association of Holbein with the Dutch. Douce reports, "It is not a little remarkable, that so late as the year 1654, there appeared a Dutch book, printed at Antwerp, where this [unknown] artist worked, entitled, 'Doodt vermaskert or Death masked,' accompanied with 18 cuts of the Dance of Death, which in the title page are ascribed to Holbein." "Notes," 19.

These instances gave rise to the popular notion that the Dance of Death was a Dutch idea. Thus we find Dickens on several occasions referring to "the old Dutch series," by which he means the Dance of Death. But the "old Dutch" series was in fact German—Platte Deutsch, perhaps.

Another association of the Dance of Death with the mistakenly named Dutch occurs in Bewick's *Interpretation of Holbein* (London: T. Hodgson, 1789). In the notes Bewick quotes a Dr. Nugent describing a Dance of Death painted in Lubec. "The Intention of the Artist was to shew that Death pays no Regard to Age or Condition, which is more particularly expressed in the Verses underneath. They were composed at first in Plat Deutsch, or Low Dutch..." Bewick's version of the Dance was another popular edition. If both he and Douce make associations between the Dutch and the Dance, ordinary readers were likely to be making the same connections.

13. Without elaborating the particular parallels, Stephen C. Gill has noted a suggestion of the Dance of Death in this scene. "Allusion in *Bleak House:* A Narrative Device," *Nineteenth-Century Fiction,* 22 (Sept. 1967), 147.

Chapter Four

1. *All the Year Round,* XVIII (27 July 1867), 120.
2. *The Grotesque in Art and Literature,* 118.
3. Dickens' last sentence was added evidently at the suggestion of Thomas Hood who, in an early review of the new serial, saw such a possibility. "Review" of *Master Humphrey's Clock, Athenaeum* (7 Nov. 1840), 887–888.

4. For an interesting discussion of Pugin's possible influence on *Martin Chuzzlewit,* see Joseph H. Gardner, "Pecksniff's Profession: Boz, Phiz, and Pugin," *The Dickensian,* 72 (May 1976), 75-86.
5. *Church and Society in England 1770-1970* (Oxford: Clarendon Press, 1976), 62.
6. 30 Jan. 1841, *Pilgrim Letters,* II, 199.
7. *Victorian Architecture* (London: Penguin, 1966), 76. See also Kenneth Clark, *The Gothic Revival* (1928; rpt. London: Pelican, 1964), 62. T.S.R. Boase says much the same in *English Art 1800-1870,* 66.
8. Henry-Russell Hitchcock says:

> In England the Picturesque and the Gothic Revival were...both, and particularly the latter...consciously nationalistic, emphasizing in an increasingly nationalistic period the recovery of local rather than of universal building traditions. For a good part of their local acceptability they were dependent, moreover, on certain warm connotations which their visual forms had for English patrons. The Rustic Cottage, the Tudor Parsonage, the Castellated Mansion had all, supposedly, been autochthonous products of the insular past.

Architecture 19th and 20th Centuries (Baltimore: Penguin, 1958), 112.

9. Visual puns on this well-known picture were common in the nineteenth century. See Nicholas Powell, *Fuseli: "The Nightmare"* (New York: Viking Press, 1973).
10. For a different, highly entertaining way of viewing the relationship between Quilp and Nell, see James Kincaid, "Laughter and Pathos: *The Old Curiosity Shop,*" in *Dickens the Craftsman,* ed. Robert B. Partlow, Jr. (Carbondale: Southern Illinois University Press, 1970), 65-94.
11. Dickens' last two novels reveal a considerable shift in this attitude. Here he shows himself deeply sensitive to the plight of the talented woman who can choose only marriage as a profession. Bella Wilfer and Rosa Bud fit the neoclassic image, but they chafe, with their creator's sanction, under the minimal roles allotted them by society. Helena Landless resembles her brother, but the resemblance is not unpleasantly androgynous.
12. J.W.T. Ley, *The Dickens Circle* (New York: Dutton and Co., 1919), 104. Edgar Allan Poe was so moved by the death he thought perhaps the reader should have been spared such pain.

> Above all, we acknowledge that the death of Nelly is excessively painful—that it leaves a most distressing oppression of spirit upon the reader—and should, therefore, have been avoided.

"The Old Curiosity Shop," 1841; rpt. *The Dickens Critics,* ed. George H. Ford and Lauriat Lane, Jr. (Ithaca: Cornell University Press, 1961), 21.

13. James Kincaid has offered an observation substantially in agreement with

the position taken here. "Dickens' attack on the mercantile organization of life in this novel is more indirect than in later novels, but it is nonetheless powerful." "Laughter and Pathos: *The Old Curiosity Shop,*" 78.

14. See Patrick Brantlinger, "Dickens and the Factories," *Nineteenth-Century Fiction,* 26 (Dec. 1971), 270–285. Brantlinger argues that Dickens was not ignorant of industrial and union problems:

    > On the contrary, it is my belief that Dickens' confusion over industrialism stems from knowledge rather than ignorance and that, in any case it leads to a definite artistic virtue—to Dickens' unique vision of society as a dismal, unfathomable tangle. 271.

15. See Robin Gilmour, "The Gradgrind School: Political Economy in the Classroom," *Victorian Studies,* XI (Dec. 1967), 205–224.
16. 30 Jan. 1855, *Nonesuch Letters,* II, 620.
17. 13 July 1854, *Nonesuch Letters,* II, 567.
18. See John Dixon Hunt, "Dickens and the traditions of graphic satire," *Encounters,* ed. John Dixon Hunt (New York: W.W. Norton, 1971), 124–155.
19. John Summerson, *Architecture in Britain 1530 to 1830* (Baltimore: Penguin, 1970), 519.
20. *The Gothic Revival,* 89.
21. *Architecture in Britain 1530 to 1830,* 516.
22. *The True Principles and Revival of Christian Architecture* (Edinburgh: John Grant, 1895), 37.
23. p. 125.
24. *Ibid.,* 126.
25. See Monroe Engel's interpretation in *The Maturity of Dickens* (Cambridge: Harvard University Press, 1959).
26. Julian Moynahan suggested that the book traces a fantasy that "is a well-nigh universal imaginative flight of childhood." "The Hero's Guilt: The Case of *Great Expectations,*" *Essays in Criticism,* X (Jan. 1960), 60–79.
27. G. Robert Stange takes this as the critical scene of the novel, and argues that the book is "conceived as a moral fable." "Expectations Well Lost: Dickens' Fable for His Time," *College English,* XVI (1954–1955), 9–17; rpt. *The Dickens Critics,* 294–308, p. 294.
28. See E. Pearlman's interesting study of inversion in the novel, a study not of the grotesque, but of reliance on *David Copperfield.* His observations with regard to the inconclusive ending of *Great Expectations* are especially provocative. "Inversion in *Great Expectations,*" *Dickens Studies Annual* 7 (1978), 190–202.
29. Alexander Welsh makes a similar point about Wemmick's divided life in *The City of Dickens* (Oxford: Clarendon Press, 1971), 143.
30. See the similar report of a criminal lawyer in our time. Seymour Wishman,

"A Criminal Lawyer's Inner Damage," *The New York Times* (Monday, July 18, 1977), 27.

31. "*Great Expectations* Yet Again," *Dickens Studies Annual* 2 (Carbondale: Southern Illinois University Press, 1972), 286.

Chapter Five

1. Charles Kostelnick sees Durdles as "a satiric caricature of Ruskin's Gothic workman." "Dicken's Quarrel with the Gothic: Ruskin, Durdles, and *Edwin Drood*," *Dickens Studies Newsletter*, 8 (Dec. 1977), 104–108.
2. 25 Oct. 1864, *Nonesuch Letters*, III, 402.
3. The manuscript version of this passage clearly contrasts inner with outer. For the passage, "In the free outer air," Dickens had written "Outisde"; for "In the Cathedral," the manuscript had "Inside." *The Mystery of Edwin Drood*, ed. Margaret Cardwell (Oxford: Clarendon Press, 1972), 73, notes 6 and 8.

List of Works Consulted

Altholz, Josef L. *The Mind and Art of Victorian England.* Minneapolis: University of Minnesota Press, 1976.

Antal, Frederick. *Hogarth and His Place in European Art.* London: Basic Books, 1962.

Arnheim, Rudolph. *Visual Thinking.* Berkeley: University of California Press, 1969.

Axton, William, "*Great Expectations* Yet Again," *Dickens Studies Annual,* 2. Carbondale: Southern Illinois University Press, 1972.

Bayley, John. "*Oliver Twist:* 'Things as They Really Are,' " *Dickens: A Collection of Critical Essays.* Ed. Martin Price. Englewood Cliffs: Prentice-Hall, 1967.

Bell, Quentin. *Victorian Artists.* Cambridge: Harvard University Press, 1967.

Bewick, Thomas. *Interpretations of Holbein.* London: T. Hodgson, 1789.

Boase, T.S.R. *English Art 1800–1870.* Oxford: Clarendon Press, 1959.

Brantlinger, Patrick. "Dickens and the Factories," *Nineteenth-Century Fiction,* 26 (Dec. 1971), 270–285.

Bredsdorff, Elias. *Hans Andersen and Charles Dickens; A Friendship and its Dissolution.* Copenhagen: Rosenkilde and Bagger, 1956.

Browne, Edgar. *Phiz and Dickens.* London: James Nisbet and Co., 1913.

Burke, Joseph and Caldwell, Colen. *Hogarth: The Complete Engravings.* New York: H.N. Abrams, 1970.

Charles Dickens, An Exhibition to commemorate the centenary of his death. London: Victoria and Albert Museum, 1970.

Child, Harold. "Caricature and the Literature of Sport: *Punch,*" *Cambridge History of English Literature.* Ed. A.W. Ward and A.R. Waller. Cambridge University Press, 1932. XIV, 212–239.

Clark, James M. *The Dance of Death.* London: Phaidon, 1947.

Clark, Kenneth. *The Gothic Revival.* London: Pelican, 1964. (first pub. 1928).

Clayborough, Arthur. *The Grotesque in English Literature.* Oxford: Clarendon Press, 1965.

Cohen, Jane Rabb. "Dickens and His Original Illustrators," Harvard: unpub. dissertation, 1968.

Coleman, B.I. *The Idea of the City in 19th-century Britain.* London: Routledge and Kegan Paul, 1973.

Colvin, Sidney. "English Painters and Painting in 1867," *Fortnightly Review,* VIII, n.s. II (Oct. 1867), 464–476.

Conrad, Peter. *The Victorian Treasure House.* London: Collins, 1973.

Cruikshank, George. *The Bottle.* London: David Bogue, 1847.

Dickens, Charles. "An Idea of Mine," *Household Words,* XVII (13 Mar. 1858), 416–417.

_______. *Collected Papers.* 2 vols. Bloomsbury: Nonesuch Press, 1937.

_______. *The Complete Novels.* Oxford Illustrated Edition. London: Oxford University Press, 1947–1957.

_______. *The Letters of Charles Dickens.* Nonesuch edition. 3 vols. Ed. Walter Dexter. Bloomsbury: Nonesuch Press, 1938.

_______. *The Letters of Charles Dickens.* Pilgrim edition. 4 vols. to date. Ed. Madeline House and Graham Storey. Oxford: Clarendon Press, 1965--

_______. *The Mystery of Edwin Drood.* Ed. Margaret Cardwell. Oxford: Clarendon Press, 1972.

_______. "Portraits," *All the Year Round,* XIV (19 Aug. 1865).

_______. *Reprinted Pieces.* Ed. B.W. Matz, London: Chapman and Hall, 1908.

_______. *The Speeches of Charles Dickens.* Ed. K.J. Fielding. Oxford: Clarendon Press, 1960.

_______. *The Uncollected Writings of Charles Dickens: Household Words.* Ed. Harry Stone. Bloomington: University of Indiana Press, 1968.

Donoghue, Denis. "The English Dickens and *Dombey and Son, Dickens Centennial Essays.* Ed. Ada Nisbet and Blake Nevius. Berkeley: University of California Press, 1971.

Dyson, A.E. "*The Old Curiosity Shop:* Innocence and the Grotesque," *Critical Quarterly,* VIII (1966).

Engel, Monroe. *The Maturity of Dickens.* Cambridge: Harvard University Press, 1959.

Engravings by Hogarth. Ed. Sean Shesgreen. New York: Dover, 1973.

Fielding, Henry. *Joseph Andrews.* Boston: Houghton-Miflin, 1961.

Findlay, L.M. "Aspects of Analogy: The Changing Role of the Sister Arts Tradition in Victorian Criticism," *English Studies in Canada,* III (1978).

Fletcher, Angus. *Allegory, The Theory of a Symbolic Mode.* Ithaca: Cornell University Press, 1964.

Ford, George H. and Lane, Lauriat, Jr. ed. *The Dickens Critics.* Ithaca: Cornell University Press, 1961.

Forster, John. *The Life of Charles Dickens.* Ed. J.W.T. Ley. London: Cecil Palmer, 1928.

Frith, William Powell. *My Autobiography and Reminiscences.* 3 vols. London: R. Bentley, 1887.

Gardner, Joseph H. "Pecksniff's Profession: Boz, Phiz, and Pugin," *The Dickensian,* 72 (May 1976). 75-86.

Garis, Robert. *The Dickens Theatre.* Oxford: Clarendon Press, 1965.

George, M. Dorothy. *From Hogarth to Cruikshank: Social Change in Graphic Satire.* New York: Walker and Co., 1967.

Gilmour, Robin. "The Gradgrind School: Political Economy in the Classroom," *Victorian Studies,* XI (Dec. 1967).

Gill, Stephen C. "Allusion in *Bleak House:* A Narrative Device," *Nineteenth-Century Fiction,* 22 (Sept. 1967).

Gilpin, William. *An Essay Upon Prints.* (London: printed for J. Robson, 1768).

_______. *Three Essays.* London: printed for R. Blamir, 1792.

Gloag, John. *Victorian Taste.* London: A. and C. Black, 1962.

Gombrich, E.H. *Meditations on a Hobby Horse.* London: Phaidon, 1963.

Hagstrum, Jean. *The Sister Arts.* Chicago: University of Chicago Press, 1958.

Hardy, Barbara. *The Moral Art of Dickens.* London: Athlone Press, 1970.

Harvey, John R. *Victorian Novelists and Their Illustrators.* London: Sidgwick and Jackson, 1970.

Hazlitt, William. *The Complete Works of William Hazlitt.* Ed. P.P. Howe. London: J.M. Dent, 1930.

_______. *The Miscellaneous Works.* London: G. Routledge and Sons, 1887.

Hewison, Robert. *John Ruskin: The Argument of the Eye.* London: Thames and Hudson, 1976.

Hitchcock, Henry-Russell. *Architecture 19th and 20th Centuries.* Baltimore: Penguin, 1958.

Hogarth, William. *Anecdotes of William Hogarth.* Ed. J.B. Nichols. London: J.B. Nichols, 1833.

Holbein, Hans. *The Celebrated Hans Holbein's Alphabet of Death.* Paris: printed for Edwin Tross, 1856.

_______. *The Dance of Death by Hans Holbein the Younger.* New York: Dover, 1971.

_______. *The Dance of Death.* Ed. F. Douce. London: John Harding, 1804.

_______. *Holbein's Dance of Death and Bible Woodcuts.* New York: Sylvan Press, 1947.

Hollingsworth, Keith, *The Newgate Novel, 1830-1847.* Detroit: Wayne State University Press, 1963.

Hood, Thomas. "Review" of *Master Humphrey's Clock, Athenaeum* (7 Nov. 1840).

Horne, R.H. "Charles Dickens," *A New Spirit of the Age.* London: Smith, Elder and Co., 1844.

Hunt, John Dixon. "Dickens and the Traditions of Graphic Satire," *Encounters.* Ed. John Dixon Hunt. New York: W.W. Norton, 1971.

Hussey, Christopher. *The Picturesque.* London: G.P. Putnam, 1927.

Jarrett, David. "The Fall of the House of Clennam: Gothic Conventions in *Little Dorrit,*" *The Dickensian,* 73 (Sept. 1977).

Johnson, Edgar. *Charles Dickens, His Tragedy and Triumph.* 2 vols. New York: Simon Schuster, 1952.

Johnson, Wendell Stacy. "The Bride of Literature: Ruskin, the Eastlakes, and mid-Victorian Theories of Art," *Victorian Newsletter* (Fall, 1964).

Jordan, Robert F. *Victorian Architecture.* London: Penguin, 1966.

Kayser, Wolfgang. *The Grotesque in Art and Literature.* Trans. Ulrich Weisstein. Bloomington: Indiana University Press, 1963. (first pub. 1957).

Kettle, Arnold. *An Introduction to the English Novel.* 2 vols. London, 1951.

Kincaid, James. "Laughter and Pathos: *The Old Curiosity Shop,*" *Dickens the Craftsman.* Ed. Robert B. Partlow. Carbondale: Southern Illinois University Press, 1970. 65–94.

Kostelnick, Charles. "Dickens's Quarrel with the Gothic: Ruskin, Durdles, and *Edwin Drood;*" *Dickens Studies Newsletter,* 8 (Dec. 1977). 104–108.

Kurtz, Leonard Paul. *The Dance of Death and the Macabre Spirit in European Literature.* New York: Columbia University Press, 1934.

Lamb, Charles. "On the Genius and Character of Hogarth." *Anecdotes of William Hogarth.* Ed. J.B. Nichols. London; J.B. Nichols, 1833.

Lane, Lauriat. "Mr. Pickwick and the Dance of Death," *Nineteenth-Century Fiction,* 14 (Sept. 1959).

Leavis, F.R. *"Dombey and Son," Sewanee Review,* 70 (1962), 177–201.

Lee, Rensselaer W. "Ut Pictura Poesis: The Humanistic Theory of Painting," *Art Bulletin,* XXII (Dec. 1940). rpt. New York: Norton, 1967.

Ley, J.W.T. *The Dickens Circle.* New York: Dutton and Co., 1919.

Lister, Raymond. *Victorian Narrative Paintings.* London: Museum Press Ltd., 1966.

Lister, T.H. "Dicken's Tales," *Edinburgh Review,* LXVIII (Oct. 1838).

Maas, Jeremy. *Victorian Painters.* London: Barrie and Jenkins, 1970.

Mâle, Emile. *L'Art Religieux de la Fin du Moyen Age en France.* Paris: 1925.

Manning, Sylvia. *Dickens as Satirist.* New Haven: Yale University Press, 1971.

Marten, Harry P. "Exaggerated Character: A Study of the Works of Dickens and Hogarth," *Centennial Review,* 20 (1976).

———. "The Visual Imaginations of Dickens and Hogarth: Structure and Scene," *Studies in the Novel,* (Summer 1974).

Mayhew, Henry. *London Labour and the London Poor.* London: Griffin, Bohn, and Co., 1861.

Miller, J. Hillis and Borowitz, David. *Charles Dickens and George Cruikshank.* Los Angeles: William Andrews Clark Memorial Library, 1971.

Moynahan, Julian. "The Hero's Guilt: The Case of *Great Expectations,*" *Essays in Criticism,* X (Jan. 1960), 60–79.

Nisbet, Ada and Nevius, Blake, ed. *Dickens Centennial Essays.* Berkeley: University of California Press, 1971.

Norman, E.R. *Church and Society in England 1770–1970.* Oxford: Clarendon Press, 1976.

Partlow, Robert B. Jr., ed. *Dickens the Craftsman.* Carbondale: Southern Illinois University Press, 1970.

Paulson, Ronald. *Hogarth's Graphic Works.* 2 vols. New Haven: Yale University Press, 1965.

________. *Hogarth: His Life, Art and Times.* New Haven: Yale University Press, 1971.

Pearlman, E. "Inversion in *Great Expectations,*" *Dickens Studies Annual,* 7 (1978), 190–202.

Perugini, Kate. "Charles Dickens as a Lover of Art and Artists," *Magazine of Art* (1903).

Pevsner, Nikolaus. *The Englishness of English Art.* London: Penguin, 1964. (first pub. 1956).

Poe, Edgar Allan, *"The Old Curiosity Shop,"* 1841; rpt. *The Dickens Critics.* Ed. George H. Ford and Lauriat Lane, Jr. Ithaca: Cornell University Press, 1961.

Powell, Nicholas. *Fuseli: "The Nightmare."* New York: Viking Press, 1973.

Praz, Mario. *The Hero in Eclipse in Victorian Fiction.* Trans. Angus Davidson. London: Oxford University Press, 1956.

Price, Martin. "The Picturesque Moment," *From Sensibility to Romanticism.* Ed. Frederick W. Hilles and Harold Bloom. New York: Oxford University Press, 1965.

Price, Uvedale. *A Dialogue on the Distinct Characters of the Picturesque and the Beautiful, in Answer to the Objections of Mr. Knight.* London, 1801.

Pugin, Augustus Welby. *An Apology for the Revival of Christian Architecture in England.* Edinburgh: John Grant, 1895.

________. *Contrasts.* New York: Humanities Press, 1969. (first pub. 1836; second edition 1841).

________. *The True Principles and Revival of Christian Architecture.* Edinburgh: John Grant, 1895.

Redgrave, Richard and Samuel. *A Century of British Painters.* Ed. Ruthven Todd. London: Phaidon Press, 1947.

Roos, David A. "Dickens at the Royal Academy of Arts: A New Speech and Two Eulogies," *The Dickensian,* 73 (May 1977).

Rossetti, William Michael. Marginal notes on Beinecke Library copy of *Expli-*

cation des Ouvrages de Peinture, Sculpture, Gravure, Lithographie et Architecture des Artists Vivants Etrangers et Francais. Paris, 1855.

_______. *Fine Art, Chiefly Contemporary.* London: Macmillan, 1867.

Rowlandson, Thomas and Combe, William. *The English Dance of Death.* 2 vols. London: Methuen and Co., 1903.

Rowlandson, Thomas. *Rowlandson's Drawings for the English Dance of Death.* San Marino, California: Huntington Library, 1966.

_______. and Combe, William. *The Tour of Dr. Syntax in Search of the Picturesque.* London: 1809.

Ruskin, John. *The Complete Works.* 39 vols. Ed. E.T. Cook and Alexander Wedderburn. London: George Allen, 1903–1912.

Saywood, B.C. "Dr. Syntax: A Pickwickian Prototype?" *The Dickensian,* 66 (Jan. 1970), 24–29.

Stange, G. Robert. "Expectations Well Lost: Dickens's Fable for His Time," *College English,* XVI (1954–1955), 9–17.

Steegman, John. *The Rule of Taste from George I to George IV.* London: Macmillan, 1936.

Stegemeier, Henri. *The Dance of Death in Folksong.* University of Chicago dissertation, 1939.

Steig, Michael. "*Dombey and Son* and the Railway Panic of 1845," *The Dickensian,* 67 (Sept. 1971).

Stone, Harry. "The Novel as Fairy-Tale: Dickens' *Dombey and Son,*" *English Studies,* XLVII (Feb. 1966), 1–27.

Stonehouse, J.H. ed. *Catalogue of the Library of Charles Dickens from Gadshill.* London: Piccadilly Fountain Press, 1935.

Summerson, John. *Architecture in Britain 1530 to 1830.* Baltimore: Penguin, 1970. (first pub. 1953).

_______. *A New Description of Sir John Soane's Museum.* London: 1955.

_______. *Victorian Architecture in England.* New York: Norton, 1971.

Van Ghent, Dorothy. "The Dickens World: A View from Todgers's," *Sewanee Review,* 58 (1950), 419–426.

Varma, D.P. *The Gothic Flame.* London: Arthur Barker, 1957.

Vogler, Richard. "*Oliver Twist:* Cruikshank's Pictorial Prototypes," *Dickens Studies Annual,* II (1972). 98–118.

Wark, Robert A. "Notes," *Rowlandson's Drawings for the English Dance of Death.* San Marino, California: Huntington Library, 1966.

Warthin, Aldred Scott. *The Physician of the Dance of Death.* New York: Arno Press, 1977; first pub. 1931.

Welsh, Alexander. *The City of Dickens.* Oxford: Clarendon Press, 1971.

Index